Happy Retirement

Carol Hagland is a retired consultant clinical psychologist. She worked as a chartered clinical, forensic, and neuro-psychologist in the NHS for over thirty years, and lectured at the Open University. She is the author of two previous books, on Asperger Syndrome and risk assessment.

HAPPY RETIREMENT

*Simple ways to transform
your relationships, self-esteem,
and emotional well-being*

Carol Hagland

ONEWORLD
OXFORD

A Oneworld Paperback Original

Published by Oneworld Publications 2011

Copyright © Carol Hagland 2011

The moral right of Carol Hagland to be identified as the
Author of this work has been asserted by her in accordance
with the Copyright, Designs and Patents Act 1988

ISBN 978–1–85168–763–3

Typeset by Jayvee, Trivandrum, India
Cover design by Jamie Keenan
Printed and bound by TJ International

Oneworld Publications
185 Banbury Road, Oxford, OX2 7AR, England

Learn more about Oneworld. Join our mailing list to
find out about our latest titles and special offers at:

www.oneworld-publications.com

Contents

Contents

Introduction

'To be able to fill leisure intelligently is the last product of civilization, and at present very few people have reached this level.'

Bertrand Russell

In earlier times, and in fact until relatively recently, people did not expect to live more than a few years after retirement. Jobs were often physically hard work, and retirement was seen perhaps as a well-earned holiday after a lifetime of work. However, the current generation of newly retired pensioners are fitter and healthier, and many can expect to live into their eighties and beyond. In addition, there are a lot more of them. The so-called 'baby-boomers' (the generation born just after the Second World War) have changed things at every stage of their lives. Now they are going to change retirement.

Many people are also retiring earlier, at fifty, fifty-five or sixty. This may be by choice, or they may be 'encouraged' to do so by employers who are downsizing. Some keep on working until sixty-five, but even at that age, these pensioners can expect to live another fifteen to twenty years on average. Those who retire earlier will, of course, have even longer. Not only does this long retirement period have financial implications, it also has other implications that are less recognized. If one retires at sixty, with a probable life expectancy of twenty to twenty-five years, retirement suddenly becomes a different prospect. It is no longer a brief holiday before you die of old age and exhaustion. It is a whole new section of life, which needs to be planned for and adjusted to.

In this book I will be asking what retirement might mean for those approaching retirement age, or those who have recently retired. Retirement, however positively embraced, means major changes are going to take place. These changes will affect relationships, self-image, money, status and possibly health. It is relatively easy to plan for retirement in the short term, and many people consider their finances quite carefully before retiring. However, fewer of them consider exactly how retirement is going to affect them emotionally and psychologically.

There are lots of books and courses available that consider the financial aspects of retirement. Many people think about this aspect of retirement as the most important, and obviously money and income must be considered. You need to try and make sure that you will be well provided for, so you should read those books too. Do your sums carefully and seek professional advice about investments. If your income is simply not going to be enough to meet your needs, then you will have to include some kind of work in your overall plan for retirement. However, money, while important, is not the key to a successful retirement. There are many ways to have a happy and fulfilled life without a huge income, but it requires planning.

So this book is not concerned primarily with money. I want to look instead at the psychological and emotional aspects of retirement. Change is always a challenge, and we cope better on some occasions than others. But you can adapt to the changes that retirement brings in a positive and constructive way, so that you enter this new phase of life ready to make the most of it.

Throughout this book, you will be asked to make notes and lists to help you make your decisions, so you may wish to find a notebook and pen before you start reading. If you organize it well, retirement can indeed be the time of your life!

1

Planning for Retirement

So you have decided to retire, or perhaps you have just done so. Are you ready for this? Retirement is changing: it is no longer the end of life. It is a time to make changes and go in new directions. What is this new retirement going to mean for you? What are you going to do?

The most important thing to realize is that this is not just another holiday that happens to be longer than usual. Retirement is the next phase of your life, and is as much of a transition as the change from teenage years to adulthood, or from being single to being married.

It may be that you had not intended to retire yet, but it has been forced upon you. Or maybe you have been planning your escape for years, and have finally made it. Perhaps you are still just thinking about it, and are not sure whether to take the plunge.

Retirement can be a lonely process. Nobody else can do it for you. In addition to your financial planning, you should discuss your plans in detail with those close to you, before you make any decisions. This is particularly important if you and your spouse are suddenly going to be spending a lot more time together. The nature of your relationship will change for both of you, and you need to be sure that you are both ready for the changes. Can your relationship cope?

We shall work through the process of adapting to retirement, looking at what it means for you. Retirement can be an opportunity to fulfil your dreams, or move in completely new directions. Perhaps you have always wanted to live abroad, or travel. Maybe you have always wanted to run your own business. Whatever retirement means for you, now is your chance to make it happen. More importantly, if you don't do it now, you will never do it.

If you don't have any particular dreams, then perhaps you need to spend a little time just freewheeling, while you rest and recuperate. Spend that time exploring what is on offer, both locally and nationally. Consider what kinds of activities you do now that you enjoy. Talk to others about their interests and activities. Think back over your life, and consider what you have enjoyed most. This could be in a work setting or during your leisure time. Think back to schooldays, teenage years and adult life. When were you happiest and why? What didn't work for you? What made you unhappy or stressed? What, if anything, would you like to do again? Who have you always admired and why? Can you copy what they have done?

Doing Nothing Forever!

If you have had a really stressful, demanding job, it may be that your idea of the perfect retirement is to do nothing forever. No more getting up with the alarm clock. No more commuting to work. No more traffic jams. No more having to do what other people want you to do. You can spend every morning in bed if you want to, and when you get up, it doesn't matter what you wear, or what you do. Heaven!

Many people do feel like this when they first retire. Often they will spend a few weeks or months making the most of this new freedom. However, there are also disadvantages to this style of life. Life ceases to have any real structure or goals, and there are few challenges. While initially this may seem like heaven, it can become rather tedious after a while.

Nevertheless, particularly if you have had a very demanding job, then it is probably wise to allow yourself a period to do this kind of chilling out when you first retire. This will enable you to wind down, and recover. It will also give you a space to think about what you would really like to do, if you haven't already done that.

It is often said that when you approach death, you regret the things that you did not do, rather than what you actually did. If this is so, then it makes sense to take the opportunity that you now have, and see if you can use your retirement phase to try and make your dreams a reality. Can you afford it? What are the risks? Are they risks that you are prepared to take? What are the possible disadvantages? What can you do about them?

For example, studies of newly retired people have found that those who move to a different part of the country after they retire sometimes find it harder to settle than those who stay in a familiar area. This is often because it becomes harder to make new friends as you get older, and by moving away, you have left your old friends behind. This doesn't mean that you should not do it, but maybe you need to think ahead. A relocation of this kind is more likely to work if you have family and friends already in the area, or if you are planning to settle in a place you already know well, or where you are sure you can make plenty of new contacts.

Assessing Your Life

Faced with the possibility of living anything up to thirty, or even forty years after retirement, it is clear that retirement for this coming generation of pensioners will be different. It can be thought of, perhaps, as part three of your life. Part one is your youth, when you gain your education and establish yourself as an adult in society. This takes perhaps twenty or thirty years. Part two is when you establish yourself in a career, or found your family, or more commonly, do both. This phase probably takes another thirty years or so. Now, as a person approaching retirement, or newly retired, you are entering part three of your life, the last phase. Nowadays, this may also be another twenty or thirty years. To make the most of this phase, you need to plan. Part of this will be financial, but your plan also needs to take account of you as an individual, your needs, your health, your likes and dislikes and your dreams or goals. You need to look at your life, both past and present, and decide where you are going next.

To begin with, you need to think about who you are or

were as a working person. What activities gave you most satisfaction during your working life? What did you hate? What do you think you will miss most? These answers will give you some indications of what you may need to try and replace once you do not have your work to fill your time. It is crucial to realize that going to work is not just about earning money, important though that is. Work offers a range of satisfactions, most of which you may have never really thought about. Many people only realize that they were there once they are gone. What kinds of things? Well, things such as your sense of yourself, your identity, your status, your social circle, intellectual challenges and, of course, money. Once retired these will change or disappear from your life. How are you going to deal with all these changes? How will you make sure that retirement for you is a positive rather than negative experience?

Who or What Will You Be as a Pensioner?

In facing the coming changes, you need to know yourself, and have some idea of the kinds of challenges that retirement will bring. Some of them will come from other people and situations. Some will come from within you. You cannot plan realistically unless you start by looking critically at yourself and your circumstances. Similarly, you cannot plan for the future unless you have some idea of where you want to go, or what you want to be.

You need to think about whether you are the kind of person who just wants to relax and enjoy life, or whether you want new challenges. You might want to continue working in some way. Some people feel that they do not want to stop working completely. This may be for very positive reasons; it may be a necessity, but it may also reflect a fear of change. However, there is no doubt that many of those who live longest are often those who keep on doing a job that they enjoy.

Sometimes the need to carry on working is tied up with a person's self-image. They do not want to accept that as they get older they might be seen by others as past it. Keeping a foothold in the workplace may seem to be the best way of avoiding this fate. On the other hand, if you are someone who feels ready to retire, and who does not particularly enjoy their job, then you probably want to stop work as soon as possible. If finances allow, then start to plan your escape now!

Whatever plan you develop cannot be put into action without considering its effect on your partner, or indeed on other family members, if there are others living with you. If one partner retires and the other does not, this will present different challenges to the couple than if both retire together. Consider which of your close relationships are most important to you, and how you will ensure that they get the attention they need. You will need a support network, and these may be family or friends, or both. If you live alone, you may need to take more active steps to find yourself a good network.

Decide also what you really do not want to have in your life after retirement, and see if you can plan to avoid these things. It is often easier to decide what you don't want, rather than what you do. Once you have done that, then you can begin to work out what you would like to include in your new life plan. Note down what your biggest worries are. Is it lack of money, or do you fear being bored, or perhaps lonely? Write down also what you are looking forward to. Look at what your current goals are, or might be, and think about whether you need to feel that what you are doing is important or that it will contribute to the community. Does any of the above mean that you need to think about moving house, or moving to a different area? It could be that moving to a smaller house or a cheaper area will remove a financial worry.

Do consider the views of those closest to you, but try not to let others discourage you if there is something that you really want to do. Too often the attitude of society as a whole is still that the elderly should sit quietly in the background and cause as little trouble as possible. It used to be said that children should be seen and not heard. Nowadays it can sometimes feel as if those over sixty have taken their place!

Ageism is perhaps the last socially accepted prejudice, although it is now illegal in the UK. Younger people still tend to see older people as boring, lacking in ability and in need of care. Some younger people will not bother to be sociable with older neighbours, because they see them as having nothing to offer. Some employers will still discriminate against older people.

Recent legislation will ensure that this is going to change. Indeed, there are signs of change already. Some employers have begun to realize the value of older workers, who tend to be more reliable, experienced and adaptable.

They are less likely to come into work with a hangover, or to get involved in sexual entanglements which interfere with work. They often value their jobs more highly than younger workers, and will come with a range of experiences which can contribute much more than their allotted job role would suggest. Added to this, there are soon going to be more older people in society, and fewer youngsters. Thus attitudes will have to change in the workplace, and this is likely to percolate through to other areas of life.

Coming to Terms With Your Ageing Self

It can be very difficult for some people to accept the idea of retirement because for them it is intimately tied up with unflattering images of old age. Many people find it difficult to accept the signs of ageing in themselves – hence the thriving industries in plastic surgery and anti-ageing cosmetics. Our society is still very youth-oriented, and it may be hard to come to terms with increasing amounts of grey hair, lined skin and other signs of an ageing body. Accepting retirement seems to say to you and others that you are really getting old, and what you see in the mirror only confirms this view.

Of course it is not pleasant to have to face these changes. It is perhaps particularly hard for those whose appearance has always been of great importance to them. This may or may not have been in a work context. Nevertheless, if you have always been admired for your looks, it will hit hard when you begin to realize that the admiration that you have always received is beginning to fade away. While cosmetic surgery and expensive face-creams can make some improvement, the reality of ageing will not go away. Indeed, some people believe that trying hard to appear young, when it is clear to all that you are not, just seems rather pathetic. Cosmetic surgery can also result in some rather grotesque alterations to a person's features, when arguably a gently ageing face would be much more pleasing.

Perhaps a more fruitful avenue to explore would be to try and consider what aspects of yourself are really most important to the people that you truly care about. If you don't know, maybe you could ask. You might be pleasantly surprised. I should be surprised if your appearance came very high up on the list. This doesn't mean that you have to give up and slouch around in grubby clothes with unwashed hair. Caring for your appearance will make you feel better about yourself, but this does not mean that you need to try and be Peter Pan!

Sadly for women, ageing in men seems to be better accepted than it is in women, even in these days of supposed emancipation. Men are said to become distinguished as they age, while women, it seems, are destined to become fat and unattractive. Have a look around you. Is this really true? Do all elderly men look like elder statesmen? Do all elderly women look a mess? This is clearly not true. Some men and women age well, others less so. If you are unhappy with how you look as you get older, see if you can pick out someone of your own sex who represents for you an attractive older person. Consider what they do with their appearance that you might copy for yourself.

Dress in what you really like, and what makes you feel

good. It does not matter what other people think. Forget the stereotyped comments about 'mutton dressed as lamb' or similar put-downs. If you like the way you look, that is all that matters. Be your own fashion guru. Experiment with colour and style, and choose something that you really like. You don't need to worry about what the boss, or indeed anyone else, thinks any longer.

What really counts is how you feel about yourself, and whether you can have a life that you enjoy. If you are happy and fulfilled, and your body works reasonably well, then a few grey hairs and wrinkles don't seem very import-ant. If they bother you a lot, dye your hair, and save up for a facelift, and then get on with what you really want to do. Those who really care about you won't care either way. In fact they may worry more about the risks of cosmetic surgery. There certainly are some.

You may still want to grieve for the loss of your youth, but there are compensations in getting older. While your interest in sex may remain, it is likely that the desperate drive that it provided in your younger years will have mellowed, making that side of life more relaxed. For many people, the removal of the need to compete in the arena of sexuality or appearance is a relief.

Most people find that they care less about what others think as they get older, and this can also be hugely liberat-ing. You may feel more able to say and do what you like, without worrying about whether anyone else will disap-prove. Your experience of life and people will mean that little is entirely new to you. You will have some idea of how to cope with whatever life throws at you.

Stop thinking about ageing and retirement as the end of everything and start thinking of this stage as a new beginning, an opportunity to live a life that you have not been able to choose, or had the time to think about, while you were working. Question your own assumptions and those of others. Refuse to be defined by age alone. It does not make sense to assume that some areas of life are closed to you just because you have reached a certain birthday. Be prepared to try things out, and stretch your boundaries. You will suddenly find that rather than life ending and doors closing, there is a whole new vista opening up before you.

Questions to Ask Yourself

What will I miss about work?
How much money will I really need?
What am I looking forward to after retirement?
Will I be lonely?
How will I fill my days?
Will I be bored?
How will this affect my close relationships?
What have I always wanted to do, but never had the chance?
How will my health affect my plans?
Do I want to move house?

As we work through this book there will be more questions to ask yourself. Listed below are the areas that other people have identified as important to having a good, balanced and satisfying retirement. These, together with the above list of questions, should get you thinking.

Five Things Necessary for a Good Retirement

Studies of those who have already retired have demonstrated that for the majority of people there are at least five things that you need to include in your life to have a happy, healthy and successful retirement. When you are working, these needs, or most of them, will largely be met by your working environment and the people in it. Now you are going to have to think about fulfilling them for yourself:

1. *Social contacts* – Meeting regularly with friends and family, and developing or maintaining a network of friends, whose company you enjoy, is crucial to maintaining both your mental and physical health. A strong, happy and close marital relationship or partnership is correlated with good health in old age. Becoming involved in community activities can also help in making new friends and give you a sense of purpose and belonging. However, people vary in the amount of social contact that they need and enjoy. Do you like to spend a lot of time alone, or are you a party animal, who easily gets bored and lonely without lots of people around?
2. *Physical activities* – Walking, cycling, swimming, keep fit, yoga, dancing, gardening and even housework can all help to keep the engine ticking over, and prevent degeneration. Any kind of regular activity or sport will

help. People who keep fit can often avoid health problems such as high blood pressure, diabetes and even dementia, and may live longer. How fit are you? Could you benefit from spending more time exercising? What kind of exercise might you enjoy? Could you take up something completely new, such as Pilates or Tai Chi?

3. *Intellectual challenges* – Having a range of activities in your life that offer intellectual stimulation will prevent boredom and keep your brain fit. Learn a language, take up a new hobby, join an evening class, or teach others something that you already know. Games such as bridge or chess, especially in a competitive setting, can offer a new challenge. You might even consider enrolling for a degree course. If you have never got to grips with computers and the internet, now may be the time to try. However, whatever you choose needs to be something you will enjoy, and that you feel is worthwhile. Give it some thought and get that grey matter working!

4. *Creative activities* – Make things, learn to paint or draw, or take up pottery or sculpture. Wood-carving or wood-turning can be immensely satisfying, or you might fancy making jewellery or Christmas decorations. Even cookery can be creative if you try new recipes and experiment. Gardening and especially garden design can be creative too. Some people enjoy making toys or models. It does not matter what it is, or even if you are not very good at it, as long as you enjoy it, and are pleased with what you create. If you have never done anything creative before, you might want to join a class

to learn a new skill. You may also make some new friends.

5. *A passion* – Something that makes you want to get up in the morning. It may be a new job, or an old hobby, such as golf or gardening. It might be a completely new interest. Many people find a new course of study opens the door to a new fascination. Some people have always dreamt of being their own boss, and running their own business. Or maybe it will be travelling that offers new experiences and excitement. Creative pursuits can also be a passion, as can involvement in community activities or politics. Could you become a local councillor, or even an MP? What will *your* passion be?

This may all sound a bit daunting at first, but as we consider the different parts of your life, and look at what kind of person you are, it should gradually become apparent to you what sort of retirement will work for you. Probably there are several possible paths you could take. If you are not sure, then experiment. Try things out, and if they feel wrong then you don't need to continue. You are in charge now, to a large extent, so make the most of it.

2

Who Am I?

Whether working or not, you are still the same person as you have always been, and you still have the skills and abilities that you have always had. Your personality has been developed over the course of your life, and has been shaped by your innate qualities interacting with your life experiences. There will be some aspects of you which are almost impossible to change, and it can be helpful to recognize what these are. Other aspects of your personality will have been learned, and there may be some scope for changing or modifying these. However, bear in mind that you have been the way you are for a good many years now, and changing will not be easy. However, it is possible, with effort, if that is what you want to do.

Think about the experience, skills and strengths that you brought to your work. Now you need to bring them to bear on your retirement.

Retirement is a real challenge to your sense of who you are. Familiar roles and familiar surroundings are lost. Everything seems to change at once. At worst, retiring can mean that because money suddenly becomes tight, and former habits have to be abandoned, you find you cannot keep up with your former friends. You may not be able to afford the expensive holidays and smart cars that you once shared with them. Even if money is not the issue, it may be that you find you have lost the common ground that you used to have. Once removed from the day-to-day bustle of work, you may struggle to find things to talk about, and friendships can wither and die as a result.

Work defines us. At a party, new acquaintances will ask, 'What do you do?' What they really want to know is where you fit into the social pattern. A job title enables people to know how to react to us, to have some idea of how well off we are, how well educated we are, and whether they are likely to share interests with us. However, it is important to realize that we are not just our job. It is not really correct to say 'I am a teacher'. In fact what you should say is 'I work as a teacher'. You are many more things than just a teacher, even if that role feels central to your life. In adjusting to retirement it is important to get in touch with all the other things you are, and look at which parts of you can begin to develop in ways that they could not do when you were working.

Work gives our lives a framework, a ready-made social group, a set of goals, a degree of status, a future and an identity. Retirement takes all that away at a stroke. If you go from a full-time, nine-to-five job to total retirement overnight, as many people do, it is no wonder that it can feel as if the rug has been pulled from under you. It is perhaps not surprising that many retired people continue to refer to their former occupation as a way of retaining their identity. 'I am a retired accountant', you might hear someone say. This maintains their sense of their own identity and still allows others to neatly pigeonhole them on first meeting. Similarly, many people remain members of their professional body after retiring, so that they can stay in touch with their previous life.

Even if you were not a professional person, you will still have had a clear identity at work – a milkman, a shop-worker, a gardener, a postman, etc. Each label carries with it a set of expectations and a clear role, which means something to everyone. Retirement takes that away, and at first the only obvious alternative is to say 'I am a pensioner'. Not surprisingly, few people feel that they want that as their only identity. To be a pensioner probably conjures up images of dowdy, down-at-heel, grey-haired and possibly infirm old folks, shuffling round the shops in baggy clothes. Hardly surprising that it doesn't appeal! However, what is obvious in recent years is that many pensioners are not accepting that image at all. They remain lively, fit and cheerful, and steadfastly ignore their ageing bodies and greying hair. Some still sport the pony-tails or the brightly dyed hair of their youth. They will often acknowledge that they cannot do all that they could when young, but that does not stop them doing what they can do now. The modern image of the pensioner is changing rapidly, and it will continue to change.

Increasingly, there are more and more pensioners who simply refuse to be defined by age. Blessed with the benefits of a welfare society that worked (for a while at least), they have had a better diet, better medical care, and better education while growing up than any generation before them. They are living longer and staying fitter. Moreover, there are a lot of them. In economic terms they are a force to be reckoned with. Alongside that is the fact that in recent years, birth rates have fallen, so the baby-boomers are now probably the biggest and most economically powerful group in society. If they refuse to accept the attitudes towards old age and retirement that used to exist, then it is certain that those attitudes will change. It is happening already.

One thing that psychology has demonstrated over and over, is that what happens to you will largely be the result of what you expect. If you expect your life to be limited and miserable, then it probably will be. If you expect to be able to keep fit and active into old age, then you probably will. Of course, sudden illness can strike anyone, but there is no doubt that the more you do, the more you are likely to be able to do. If you say 'I can't', then you will not be able to. If you sit in your chair watching TV all day, you will soon find it difficult to get out of that chair. Muscles waste with disuse alarmingly quickly, and in order to keep your body healthy you need to exercise it.

Feeling Useful

You may have worked in a job that meant that you always felt useful and needed. This may be very important to you. If so, you may find that once you have retired you want to find another opportunity to make a useful contribution. Much depends on how important it is to you to feel needed and useful, and there are, of course, many different ways of making a useful contribution to society. It might be that you would prefer a role that is less demanding than your present job. Sometimes, after a lifetime of helping others, you may feel ready to do something completely different.

While some people relax into retirement with a sigh of relief, there are others who are left feeling that society is telling them that they are finished, and no longer able to contribute. Not surprisingly, such ideas are likely to lead to feelings of worthlessness and depression. Are these your thoughts when faced with retirement?

You need to challenge such unhelpful thoughts if you are to avoid the depression trap. You can contribute and be useful, even if you stop working for money. Many, many voluntary organizations will welcome your skills and experience. You may need to experiment a little, and try a few out before you find the right one, but do not allow these negative thoughts to overwhelm you. You are not finished unless you choose to be.

Even if you don't want to become a formal volunteer, it may well be that you have neighbours or family members who would welcome some extra help with open arms: elderly parents who are struggling to cope alone; children with their own children who would be so grateful for help with childcare; elderly or disabled neighbours who would love to have some company, or help with their shopping.

Of course, if poor health has been a contributory factor in your own retirement, this is bound to limit what you can offer to others. However, it is worth exploring what is needed. For example, several organizations welcome help from letter writers who will lobby their member of parliament on important issues. Some charities welcome help from knitters who can produce toys for children in need. If you can still drive, you might be able to drive those who are no longer able to do so.

The important thing is that you don't imagine that you have been 'written off'. If you are really struggling with this, consider getting some professional help. Talk to your GP. Many surgeries now have counsellors to whom you can easily be referred. There is nothing wrong with asking for help. Just because you are older, that does not mean that time spent on yourself is wasted.

Know Yourself

Self-awareness is crucial if you are to get the best from your retirement years. You need to know what kind of person you are, what you enjoy, what you hate, what makes you anxious and what frustrates you. It may help to talk to close friends and family about this. How do they see you? What strengths and weaknesses do they see you as having? Do you agree? If not, why do you think their opinion might be different? It is important that in doing this exercise, you don't get upset or angry about their feedback. They will not be able to be honest with you if you are going to fly off the handle! Bite your tongue and listen. Don't rush to defend yourself. Instead write down what they have said, and go away and think about it. Even if you don't like what you hear, is there some truth in it?

What Have You Lost?

While you were working, you may have had a particular and important role, such as a doctor or a postman. You may also have had other roles – a head of department, a health and safety officer, a trainer of others, the longest serving employee, a union representative, and so on. Find your pen and paper again, and write down the roles that you had in your work environment. There may only have been one or two, or there may have been many. Why did you have these roles? What did you get out of them? Some of them you may be heartily glad to lose. Note those down too. In deciding who you really are, you need to know what you dislike as well as what you like.

Note down also what you will miss most when you are no longer at work. Will it be your roles and status, the people, or the intellectual challenges? It may something as simple as having access to the internet or a good library. Write it all down, because this is all information that will help you decide who you are and what you want.

What Do You Still Have?

Some things will not change. You are still the same person. You probably have roles associated with your home life and leisure activities that will not change. You may no longer be the main breadwinner, but you are still a husband or wife, parent, grandparent, or even perhaps a child to your elderly parents, if they are still alive. You may be a member of the local golf club, or be involved in other sports or leisure activities. Indeed you may be able to become more involved with these activities now you are retired. You may have roles within the community, perhaps on the parish council or working with a conservation group, for example. These will still be there for you, and if you enjoy them, you may be able to take on a more active role than previously. Your relationships with your partner or friends will also still remain, although they may change as a result of retirement.

What Do You Like to Do?

Returning to your pen and paper, write down how you spend your time when not at work. If you have already retired, think back to what you did when you were working. It is likely that you valued these activities, because you made time for them even when you did have to work. Beside each activity, put down a rough estimate of how often you do these things and for how long.

Next, examine the list, and think about which of these activities you really enjoy and would like to continue. Look at what you are doing that you would prefer to give up. Now would be a good time to make changes. If a large part of your time is spent watching TV or drinking in the local pub, then perhaps you need to think about how these activities will fit into your new life. Spending all day watching TV will make you very passive and you will probably become overweight and unhealthy. Spending longer hours in the pub is likely to be expensive, and is also bad for your health! This is not to say you should give up these activities if you enjoy them, but perhaps they need to be restricted, as they are when you are at work.

What Are Your Dreams?

Many people have dreams of what they will do when they retire, and many others have dreams of what they will do if they win the lottery. Sometimes people have nurtured a dream since childhood. Some dreams are just that, and probably impossible to realize. However, stop for a moment and ask yourself: what stops you from realizing your dream? If what has always stopped you has been the need to earn a living, then maybe retirement is the time you can finally have a go at making your dream real. Think carefully about the practicalities first, but now is the time to consider seriously whether you can. After all, life is passing by, and you only have one.

Here is a list of common dreams:

- Starting your own business
- Moving to the country
- Running a smallholding
- Moving to the seaside
- Moving abroad
- Travelling round the world
- Retraining to do something different
- Taking a degree in a subject you love
- Being an artist
- Writing a novel

Yours may completely different. That does not matter. Write them down, and then think about what would really be involved in making one or more of them real. Can you do it? What would be the problems and drawbacks? Are you willing to face these? Can you afford it? What stops you?

Next, stop and think about what your dreams were when you were a child. What did you want to be when you grew up? Have you succeeded? If not, why not? It may be, of course, that your ideas about yourself and what you want from life have changed as you have grown up. But perhaps you should revisit these early dreams and see if any of them are now still desirable, or possible. Or if they are not possible in their original form, do they give you a clue as to an area of interest that would be worth pursuing now?

Here are some common childhood dreams:

- Being an engine driver on a train
- Being an actor
- Driving racing cars
- Being a model
- Being a vet
- Being a pilot
- Running a shop

Perhaps you always wanted to be an engine driver. You might be able to realize that dream in a minor way by joining one of the many groups that maintain and run old steam trains: you might even get to drive the engines. If you fancied being on the stage, how about joining an amateur dramatics society, or registering with an agency who deals with older models? Older people are needed in advertising, just as children are.

One good place to start is with the interests you had in your childhood and adolescence. What did you like doing then? Could you revisit one or more of these old interests and develop them further? Perhaps there is something that you always wanted to do but never managed to achieve. Some of these activities may no longer be possible, of course. You may not be fit enough now to do some of the things you used to do as a youngster, or it may be simply that you have moved on, and they no longer interest you as they once did. Nevertheless, revisit them in your mind and reconsider them.

Find What You Really Enjoy Doing

Perhaps you could try something completely new. It may be that a friend is trying a new sport or interest that you could share. Listen to those around you, and you may hear people talking about interests, activities or sports that you have never thought about before. What about hang-gliding, or snow-boarding? Would you enjoy bird-watching or breeding dogs?

You could browse through the local adult education brochure and see what is on offer: something may catch your eye. You could learn about archaeology and go on a dig. You might fancy learning a new language. If you need or want to work, but want a change, you may find a training course that will help. Most of these courses will expect you to pay a fee, so be prepared for that. However, many establishments do give allowances to pensioners, so make sure that you check that out too. There are some benefits to getting older, so make the most of them!

I have already mentioned that some people dream of travelling extensively when they retire. This might be a round-the-world cruise, or simply touring with a caravan or motor-home around your own country. For some, it will be the chance to take a once-in-a-lifetime holiday. For others travelling can become a way of life, income permitting. If you want to travel regularly, then you will need to build the financial element of this into your plan. It may be that working part-time or casually will be the way you can fund your travels. There are only two limiting factors; health and money. Be sure that you can cope physically with what you are planning, make sure you can afford it, and check that you can get adequate travel insurance. The latter can become more difficult as you get older.

It is important to distinguish between being good at something, and enjoying it. It doesn't matter if you are not very good at something if you really enjoy it. What other people think does not matter a jot. If we go for a walk in the country, we don't give thought to how we do it, or whether other people would think it a good walk or a bad one – we simply enjoy the experience. Similarly you can ride, swim, cycle, paint, draw, write or anything else you fancy, for your own pleasure.

Do not allow other people's opinions to stop you doing something you love. As long as you are not harming anyone else, there is nothing wrong in doing things badly, or even modestly. You may not win prizes, but that is not what is important. Of course, if you are good at something, and you have not previously had a chance really to develop your skills, retirement may be the opportunity you have been waiting for. You will have time to work at it, and if in time you excel, then so much the better. However, it is the doing and the enjoyment that really matter.

It used to be suggested that jobs fell into four main areas of activity. One area covered those jobs that involved working with people, one area was working with numbers, one was working with things, and one was working with animals. Most people, it was felt, had a preference for one or other of these areas and this would help them to identify the kinds of jobs they might enjoy.

For example, working with people might mean that you would enjoy being a nurse, teacher, social worker, shop assistant or care worker. Working with numbers might mean you would like being an accountant, insurance salesman, bank cashier, statistician or mathematician. Working with things might mean that you would enjoy being a carpenter, a gardener, an engineer, a warehouseman, a builder or an artist. Working with animals might mean that you would want to be a vet, a kennel maid, a horse trainer or a farmer.

Of course it doesn't take much examination of these ideas to realize that it isn't that simple. A shop assistant will have to deal with numbers, as will a nurse and a teacher, while a warehouseman and a builder will have to deal with people too. Few jobs involve only one of these areas. Nevertheless, in our quest to discover what kind of person you really are, with or without a job, considering these four areas might give you some clues. Think about which would appeal to you most.

What have been your biggest achievements and challenges throughout your life, whether at work or at home? What gave you the biggest kick? What did you find most stressful or difficult? It does not matter what your answers are. All that I am trying to do here is to help you understand what you are like, and what makes you happy. One of the joys of being retired is that you are now in charge, and you can make changes, experiment and choose what you really enjoy. The only thing to beware of is making changes that are very difficult to reverse, especially if you feel uncertain about them. If you want to go and live abroad, for example, make very sure that you have a place to return to, and an income, however small, if everything goes badly wrong. Those who are naturally more cautious may never even contemplate such a major change, but if it appeals to you, then do make sure you do some careful planning first.

The Need for Contact With Others

Some jobs involve constant contact with other people, and lots of social life within work. Some jobs are quite solitary, and involve few other people. Think for a moment, not just about your last job, but about all the other jobs you have had. Were these jobs that involved being with lots of other people, or jobs that meant you worked alone? Which made you happiest? Sometimes, for reasons of need or conveni-ence, we end up in a job that does not really match our personality and may lose sight of the fact that we would actually like something different. Thinking back to earlier jobs, or even to your childhood, may help you to understand whether you are someone who needs a lot of social contact or not.

Some people prefer to work alone. They may be quite sociable in many ways, but still prefer to have a job that they can get on with on their own. Some people love being part of a team, and only really work well when they can be part of a group whose members all have the same goal. Yet others like to have some company, but would prefer to work only with one or two others. If you have to spend a whole day alone, are you content with whatever you are doing, or do you feel restless and lonely?

If you are outgoing, and enjoy meeting people, then you probably need to include activities that will get you out of the house, where you can meet others and make new friends. If, on the other hand, you are more introverted or independent and often prefer being alone, then you might like to have a quieter retirement, where you spend time in more solitary pursuits such as gardening or painting. You may still enjoy social contact but are more likely to be content with your immediate family and close friends. If you force yourself to engage in a lot of outside activities with a lot of new people, you may find this stressful and tiring.

Being Part of a Community

Most of us have some core values which are very important to our view of ourselves and how we fit into society. Some people value family ties above all others, and organize their lives so that they can spend large amounts of their time with their family members. For others, their sense of community will come from the larger group, and they will often get involved in local politics, or will become a school governor or parish councillor as a way of contributing to their local community. Others think big, and want to get involved in national movements or even international ones. Would you enjoy becoming involved in a worldwide charity organization, or a political movement such as Greenpeace?

These core values may be closely allied to what you might describe as your passion, although this is not necessarily so. However, most of us feel happier if we can identify with a social group within our community. When we are at work, we become part of a ready-made community, and when we first retire, this loss of community may be one of the most striking losses we experience. When people have travelled long distances to work and worked long hours, they may feel little sense of attachment to their local community and this can add to the sense of disconnection.

If you do not have close family around, and feel isolated at home, you will be most in need of establishing new links with others. Joining local groups of various kinds will be more important to you than to those who already have good local connections and family members nearby. You may also want to be part of a larger community by becoming involved in national politics or national charity organizations. If you are interested in becoming involved in these kinds of activities, the best place to look for information is probably the local library, which will have details of local and national branches of most well-known organizations of this kind. Ask your local librarian to help, if you are not sure where to look.

If you can obtain access to the internet, either at a library or at home, then you can easily get information of this kind by using one of the established search engines. There are a number of websites devoted to the new phase of life that retirement offers. Some of these are listed at the end of this book, but you may be able to find others. Some will offer advice about health; others will help you find work after retirement, or assist you in starting your own business. Some provide dating agencies for the older person, so if you are on your own and lonely, this may be a new avenue to explore.

If you don't know much about the internet, maybe now is the time to learn. Most local adult education services will have details of classes for beginners, and some will have special classes for older people. Again, ask the local librarian for help here. If you haven't used it before, the internet can open up a huge world of possibilities for friendship, training and information. Start exploring.

The Need for Structure

Work gives your life a structure. The day is mapped out for you, even if you have a reasonable degree of autonomy. You have to get up and be at work by a certain time, and you will probably finish at a certain time. You go to work on certain days, and are at home on other days. Although you have some freedom of choice both at work and at home, the structure imposed by work will still shape your life. Once you retire that disappears.

Some people relish this change and love the sense of freedom that it gives. Others find it anxiety-provoking, while yet others simply get bored. What are you like? If you have a holiday, do you tend to get bored? Do you have to fill your waking hours with activity? Do you feel anxious or uneasy if there is nothing planned? If someone calls on you unexpectedly, are you pleased or annoyed at being interrupted? Are you someone who likes order in your life, or do you like to be spontaneous?

If you like structure, then you may find it helpful to commit yourself to a range of activities outside the home, where there are clear expectations of what you will do and when. This can help to replace the structure that work gave you. Alternatively, you may find that you can set up a daily or weekly timetable for yourself which will fulfil your need to have structure, but which remains within your control. If, on the other hand, you are someone who relishes the freedom that retirement brings, then you can be as spontaneous as you wish. When you wake up each morning, you can ask yourself 'what shall I do today?' For you, the best course of action is probably to have a portfolio of interests and activities that you can pick up or put down as you feel inclined. You will probably not want to commit yourself to a regular volunteering role, or anything else that requires a fixed timetable.

Response to Change and Challenge

There are undoubtedly some kinds of people who enjoy novelty, change and challenge more than others. They may enjoy taking risks and trying out new ideas. Being busy, and having new challenges, is essential to them, and if they do not have a lot to do, they can become bored and depressed. Is this you? If it is, then the conventional model of a 'pipe and slippers' type of retirement is likely to fill you with horror. You will need to plan an active retirement, with goals to meet and challenges to face. You may be one of those who would love to start their own business, or perhaps to take up a new course of education or training. You might fancy a round-the-world trip. Or you might want to become involved in local politics.

Other people like a quiet life. Too many demands tend to make them stressed and anxious. It does seem that some people react more readily to stress than others, and if you are one of these, it helps to be aware of it. If the idea of changes and new challenges makes you anxious, then you are probably like this. You probably prefer to have clear goals and plenty of time to complete the necessary tasks. If this sounds like you, then make sure that you do not commit yourself to too much too soon, or you will be in danger of becoming as stressed as you may have been at work.

An Ideal Day

Can you imagine your ideal day? What would it include? A late breakfast on a sunny terrace? A swim followed by a stroll in the country and a nice pub lunch? Or are your tastes more adventurous? Do you want to go rock-climbing, or walk the Pennine Way? Or perhaps you want to go and see the Northern Lights? Is your ideal day a one-off, or is it something you see yourself doing regularly, perhaps every day?

Maybe it would be as simple as running your own little tea-room, cooking home-made cakes and chatting to your regular customers? Whatever you decide, ask yourself if it would really be as much fun as you imagine. What might be the disadvantages? For example, it might seem fun to run a café in the summer, when customers are plentiful and in holiday mood, but what about in the winter, when customers are few, and you have to get up in the cold and dark to prepare for the day? Will the rewards be enough to keep you motivated and happy? Similarly, a walk and a pub lunch will be lovely when the weather is good, but how often will you want to do this? Perhaps once a week, but probably not every day.

Nevertheless, it may still be worth having a try, and seeing how you get on. The most important thing is not to burn your boats, so that if it doesn't work out, there is still a way back. Don't sink all your money into a new long-term venture that you have not tried and tested. Put your toe in the water and try it out – don't jump in head first! In the above example, maybe you could try working in a café for a while first, and see how you like the day-to-day experience of it.

After considering your answers to all of these questions, I would hope that you are beginning to have a clear idea of what kind of person you are, how you react to changes, what you like and dislike, and what the things are that you will miss most about work. This is a further step on the road to your ideal retirement.

3

New Roles

So, we are beginning to have a picture of what kind of person you are, and what you might like to do once you have retired. It is clear that you are going to have to give up much of your old identity that came from your work, and think about developing a new sense of self, ready for this new future. This new sense of self relies on being able to establish new roles and rewards. It is about giving your life meaning and purpose. What other roles are possible? What will be most rewarding?

A retirement plan can provide you with new roles, and help to replace the losses that leaving your job may have brought. It is also important to challenge old, unhelpful ways of thinking about yourself and the future now that you have retired. Thoughts about being finished, and life being over, will not be compatible with new plans, new roles and new ideas about how your life can develop. Setting yourself new goals and working towards those goals is a sure way to begin to feel more positive and cheerful, even if you later decide to adapt or change those goals.

Retirement on Health Grounds

If you have been forced to retire for health reasons, or you are unfortunate enough to become ill soon after retiring, this can add to any difficulties in adaptation. Becoming seriously ill has a profound effect not only on your ability to do what you want, but also on your self-image. From being a capable and independent person, with a clear role in society, you are suddenly thrust into the role of a dependent, infirm and elderly person. This can feel like a huge assault on your self-esteem, and your confidence in yourself. It is not surprising that many people, when faced with such a situation, become depressed, at least temporarily.

In such a situation, it is important not to let these feelings control you. Try to avoid negative thoughts which focus on a victim role, such as 'Why has this happened to me?' 'This is not fair', 'Everything goes wrong for me' and so on. The first step is to accept that it has happened to you, and the second is to take an active approach to coping with it. Seek out information about your condition, and learn how best to manage it. Try to focus on what you can do, rather than what you can't. This is not always easy to do, but the pay-off is worth it: you will be able to make the best of what years remain to you, rather than wallowing in miserable feelings of helplessness.

Money as Part of the Plan

It is important to acknowledge that money has to be part of your plan. Before you plan anything else, you need to be sure that you can live on your pension and any investment income you may have. If not, then it is essential that earning money needs to be a part of your final plan. However, this does not necessarily mean that you have to stay in the same job, or even the same area of work. You can take a new look at how you might make money, and do something completely different.

Until recently, more people chose to give up work completely than wished to continue, but this is changing. Many people don't feel ready to give up work and accept the retired role. In addition, poorly performing investments, lack of savings and the presence of more older people in the population are likely to mean that many more people need to continue to earn at least something. An ageing population means there will be fewer young workers available, and the increased life expectancy and fitness of the older members of the community will mean that they are poised to take their place.

Part-time Working

If money is an issue, but you don't want to continue working full-time, then the simplest option is to do the same job you have always done, but do less of it. Work part-time, or as a consultant if that is possible. Do less, and take on fewer responsibilities, and thereby reduce your stress levels. Many employers would rather allow you to do that than lose you completely.

Many people find working part-time is an excellent solution. This may be achieved simply by reducing the hours you spend working for your current employer, although if you return to your previous type of job and previous employer, you may find that you are expected to squeeze most or all of what you used to do in a full-time job into a part-time one, so that you are effectively doing the same job for less money. Be very wary of falling into this trap. Get a clear statement, preferably in writing, of what your new job will entail, and make sure that it is proportionately less than you used to do. You may also find that your relationship with your colleagues changes too. Those who work full-time often look down on or resent part-timers, and because you will not be around for some of the week, you may find that you are not consulted, or included in the decision-making process in the way that you used to be. This can be very frustrating and upsetting, and you may need to be quite assertive in order to make sure that you are not forgotten. Even in those places where there is a culture of part-time working, this can still be a problem at times.

If you choose to work as a consultant, there can also be problems with former colleagues who may see you as taking the cream of the jobs and avoiding all the boring hard work. Whether this is fair or not, it is important to be aware that a consultancy role may provoke resentment in some people. You will need to be particularly tactful in such a role. It may, indeed, be easier to become a consultant in a different place, rather than trying to step back into your old working environment. Even if you stay with the same employer, a change of team or office may be wise.

Many people prefer to have a complete change, and an alternative might be looking around for part-time work which is local and not too demanding. Of course, it will need to pay sufficient to be worthwhile, and it will need to be interesting in its own right in order to be satisfying. Get into the habit of buying your local paper regularly and see what jobs are advertised there. Visit local employers and ask them if they would be willing to take on part-time workers. Ask at local employment agencies, and keep an eye on those little boards in local shop windows. People often advertise part-time employment much more informally than full-time work, so you may need to keep your eyes open in the local area for a while to find what you want.

Sometimes it can be useful to write to local companies and send your details to them 'on spec'. You may just catch them at the right time, when they are thinking of looking for additional help. Personal contacts can be very useful too: talk to people you know, and let them know you are looking for work.

Working for Yourself

Many people dream of running their own business and retirement can be a good time to start. You may have a lump sum payment from your employer, and having a regular pension can give you a financial cushion while you get the business up and running. However, if you are entering an area that is new to you, do seek advice, and do not commit your hard-earned money until you are fairly sure that you can make it work. It is all too easy to get carried away with an appealing idea, without really looking at all the possible disadvantages. You must approach the project objectively, and be certain you have explored all the angles. You may also have to put in very long hours, at least in the beginning. Rather than slowing down, you may find yourself needing to speed up! However, running your own show can be enormously rewarding and fun.

Self-employment comes in many guises, and ideally your chosen business needs to be one that will have some likelihood of long-term survival. There are many short-term ideas available, and far too many are advertised with the sole aim of parting you from your capital, so do tread carefully before you begin. Get advice, do your research and be sure that you know your market before you spend your hard-earned money. Most areas now have associations that offer support to local businesses and those wanting to start a business. You may find details of these at the local library, in the local paper or in your local town hall.

Listed below are a number of ideas that may get you started on the new road to self-employment. You should regard these simply as stimulants to new ideas. There are so many possible ways to start your own business that it is impossible to cover them all. However, once you have an idea, it is wise to look for others who have experience in this area who may be able to offer advice.

Bear in mind, too, that many small businesses will need a certain amount of capital to set them up, and you need to consider how much you can afford to invest in your idea, and whether you are going to approach the bank or some other source of funding for additional financial support. Setting up a small business from scratch is not always easy, but it can be done if you spend some time gathering information and get appropriate help first. It may be, however, that you have existing knowledge and experience that you can capitalize on to develop a business. This is perhaps the best idea, because you will already know the pitfalls. Other ideas are outlined below.

Buy an Existing Business

One possibility is to buy an existing business from someone who is moving on. This can be an excellent way of getting into a new area of business. Your premises, if needed, will already be established, as will your customer base. You should be able to get a good idea of the income and costs of such a business before you commit yourself. However, as before, do be careful of committing your cash before you are confident that what you are buying is a genuine, established business. If it sounds too good to be true, it probably is, and it begs the question 'why is the owner selling if the business is so good?' It is not always easy to find businesses for sale, but you may see them advertised in a local paper. Personal contacts can be useful, and if you join a local small business association, it is possible that you will hear of opportunities through them.

Buy a Franchise

As with an established individual business, buying a franchise can avoid many of the pitfalls and problems of setting up a business from scratch. Your business logo and image will already be known to customers, and you will have a ready-made source of supply for any materials that are needed. On the downside, there is often little flexibility in the package being sold, and a successful franchise can be very expensive to buy into, while there is no guarantee of success.

To find successful franchise opportunities, one of the best sources of information is likely to be the internet. Once again, if you are not familiar with the internet and how it works, engage the help of your local librarian. If you really do not want to do this, then some businesses will be advertised in magazines that devote themselves to business interests. However, it is worth noting that the internet has become so much a part of established business that not familiarizing yourself with its workings is likely to put you at a serious disadvantage.

Use Your Skills to Help Others

If you have particular skills or expertise in something that you enjoy doing, then you may be able to use this to undertake jobs for others. Small-scale repairs, gardening, babysitting, dressmaking, cooking and car maintenance are all examples of skills that others may be happy to pay for. Similarly a willingness to care for pets while their owners are on holiday, or even to help busy people look for a new home to buy, can all be good ways to generate income. A card in a local shop window may be all you need in the way of advertising. Once you are established, you may well find that you also get new customers by word-of-mouth recommendations.

Become a Professional Carer

If you like helping others, and are practical, then there are many opportunities to become a carer. Many elderly and disabled people need extra help, whether in residential homes or in their own homes. You could try being a carer who goes into a disabled person's home to help them with tasks they cannot manage alone. Some of these jobs can be quite physically demanding, so do be sure that you can do what is required without over-taxing your own resources. However, these kinds of jobs can be very rewarding, although they are not usually very well paid. Local papers usually carry a wealth of advertisements for caring jobs. It is the one area of work where there always seems to be a shortage of people to do the job. Bear in mind, however, that you will need to undergo vetting and checks to ensure that you are a reliable and trustworthy person. Legislation varies from country to country, but is strict in the UK.

Other Work You Can Do from Home

Unfortunately, as with business ideas, there are many sharks providing opportunities for home-working whose main motivation is to part you from your capital. As before, anything that seems too good to be true almost certainly is, and should be avoided. You will often see advertisements that ask you to send money to 'buy into' a home-working scheme. Usually these are a scam, and once they have your money little else will follow.

Most genuine home work is poorly paid to the point of being exploitative. Stuffing envelopes, or something similar, can often be done at home for a large company, but you will rarely make much money from this, and it is hardly going to enrich your life. However, you may still be able to work from home if you have a marketable skill, as with some of the odd-job ideas above, or if you can work online. Creative activities, such as dressmaking, writing, giving music lessons, pottery, woodwork and painting, can all be done at home, but you will need to put effort into marketing your products, and this is often the most difficult part.

If you decide that working from home is what you really want to do, then begin by making a list of your skills and abilities, and note down which of these you think may be saleable. There are many books available which aim to help people start their own business, and it is probably worth investing in a few of these before you start, as each will have a slightly different emphasis. There are certain minimum legal requirements and you need to know about these. For example, if people are visiting your home to make use of your services, then you may need personal liability insurance.

Extend a Hobby

You may already have a hobby that you love which could be extended into a business. You may want to breed animals, grow plants or vegetables for sale, sell something that you make, or teach your particular skill or hobby to others. You will need to do some research to find out if your idea will have a market, but this can be a very enjoyable way of earning some money to supplement your pension. You also need to make sure that you are operating within the law.

Become an Odd Job Man/woman

If you are practical, you may be able to find work doing odd jobs for people in your local area. Many builders do not want to take on very small repair jobs, while many older or busy people do not feel that they have the energy or time to do them themselves. Such people will be very glad of a reliable person who will do such jobs at a reasonable cost. You will need to think about insurance and, depending on the type of work, you will need to know about any legal regulations or limitations on what you can do. However, this may be worth exploring if you have saleable skills of this kind.

Online Trading

In recent years, the development of the internet, and companies such as eBay, have made it possible for thousands of people to set up and run small businesses from their homes, buying and selling for profit. The knack is in picking items to sell which are desirable, easy to store and not too expensive to post. A number of adult education classes now exist to help beginners learn how to use eBay and/or the internet. However, with a little common sense and experimentation, it is not difficult to master eBay once you have a nodding acquaintance with the internet. Try buying one or two low-cost items as an experiment, and then once you have received them, re-list them for sale. EBay's website explains it all, and as long as you don't buy expensive items until you have more confidence, you cannot go too far wrong. However, this is becoming an increasingly popular means of earning money, so there is a lot of competition, and you need to be aware of the various regulations that govern selling by mail order, as well as knowing what your income tax liabilities are likely to be. Careful record-keeping is important.

New Directions/Retraining

There are lots of opportunities for training and retraining later in life these days, and although you will probably have to pay for any formal courses you take, you may get a reduction in fees as a pensioner. Adult education classes and courses at local further education colleges may be worth exploring, while the Open University is second to none in providing a huge range of courses at all levels. Another option, if you can find a sympathetic employer, might be to learn on the job. A change of direction may give you a new lease of life, and will make the need to continue working much more enjoyable.

Use Your Home as a Source of Income

Your home itself may be a source of income if you approach it in a new way. One of the simplest ways to increase your income is to provide a bed and breakfast service. This assumes that you have at least one suitable spare room. However, like everything else in life, this has become more complicated in recent years and there are many more regulations around providing such a service than there used to be. Also, the expectations of the visiting public have risen, and they may be looking for en-suite accommodation and greater comfort and privacy than used to be the case. However, if this appeals to you, talk to your local council and Tourist Information Office, who should be able to advise you. Another possibility is to offer a room to rent. If you live near a college or university, there may be students who would welcome a room locally at a reasonable price. Some large companies are also keen to know of local accommodation for their new staff that are just moving into the area and may need temporary accommodation. In the UK there is a special 'Rent-a-room' scheme which allows you to charge up to a set weekly amount for the room without incurring an additional tax liability. The amount is subject to change, so check with the Inland Revenue before going ahead.

If this appeals to you, then do think about how it may feel to have a stranger living in your home. Are you adaptable, or will you find it irritating if they do things differently from you? Will you allow smokers? What about visitors? What about security? If you are living alone, you may need to be particularly careful who you take in, but you may enjoy the additional company, or just the feeling that someone else is around.

Finally, if you have an interesting or historical home, you may be able to hire it out to companies who look for film or advertisement locations. These companies do not always want anything exotic, but well-preserved, historically accurate buildings are often of interest to them. While they pay relatively well, you will have to expect a lot of people tramping around your home, and a lot of upheaval while they do their work. On the other hand, this will be for relatively short periods. This kind of work is handled by specialist agencies, but you can probably find more information online.

A Portfolio Life

More and more people, whether retired or not, are developing a way of life which includes a range of ways of earning money. This has been called the portfolio life and has the advantage that you are not dependent on a single market or customer base. The parts of the portfolio may include some home-working, some odd jobs and some part-time work for an employer. This gives you flexibility, a range of social contacts and lots of different interests, so it is well worth considering.

Getting Detailed Information

If you are inspired by any of the above ideas, you will need to get some detailed information about the area of work that interests you. There will be financial implications, legal requirements and practical considerations, and I would recommend that you look for as much information as you can before you start out on this path. There are lots of local sources of help and advice, and many books devoted to the subject. If you feel this is for you, start doing your homework first, before you jump in with both feet.

Nevertheless, there is no doubt that for many people, working for themselves is profoundly rewarding. There will certainly be no lack of challenges, but part of the fun is in working out how you will overcome the obstacles.

Replace Your Losses

If, however, you do not want to return to any kind of work, and yet you really have no ideas about what you might do with your retirement, then returning once again to the losses that retirement brings may give you some clues. Taking each of the losses in turn, we can look at the kinds of activities that might help to replace these, and this may offer another way to help you to shape your plan.

Structure

Work gives your days, weeks and months a structure and timetable that is lost when you retire. If you miss this, you can re-establish the structure in your life in several ways:

- Volunteer for something that provides a structure by way of regular demands.
- Become involved in sports or activities that have their own timetable.
- Enrol for a course of study that has its own timetable.
- Create your own timetable of activities.
- Allow demands from other family members to create a timetable for you.

Status

If your job gave you status, and a responsible or specialist role, then it can feel very hard to have that taken away from you at a stroke. However, there are roles within the community that will make use of your skills and give you a sense that you can still have influence, and make things happen. The following may be of interest:

- School governor
- Member of the parish council
- Local district councillor
- Member of the local NHS Trust advisory board
- Chair or member of a local charity group
- Chair of the local village hall management committee
- Volunteer guide in a local museum or attraction
- Volunteer in a hospital

Of course, the extent to which you can influence these groups will vary enormously, but usually these kinds of organizations are short of members who are willing to take an active role, and will welcome anyone who is keen to take on new responsibilities. If, however, you have retired because of health problems, make sure you avoid taking on too much at once. Some of these jobs can be just as demanding as a paid job.

Intellectual Challenge

For many people, their job is a source of intellectual challenge. They are presented with problems that need to be solved, or tasks that need to be planned. New skills may be learned, or old ones exercised. Many jobs include a lot of travelling, which offers its own kind of intellectual challenge as well as social stimulation. Once you have retired, you may miss these challenges, and you may need to find other ways of providing these for yourself. This is one of the reasons that so many older people choose to return to some kind of study. It doesn't matter whether you do this formally by means of taught courses, or whether you choose to find your own path, doing your own reading and research. At the very least, doing a daily crossword will keep your brain active, but there are so many alternative and exciting opportunities now available to challenge your grey matter, that it is worth visiting your local library, adult education centre or university to see what is on offer.

Find New Goals

When you are at work, your life has a structure which tends to include long-term goals and with them a sense of future. Once work is finished, there is a risk that you may feel set adrift, with no sense of future other than ultimately death. It is important, therefore, that you have some goals for your retirement. These may be your own personal goals, or they may be imposed by others when you take on one or more of the roles outlined so far. Whichever you choose, make sure that you are happy with them, and that they give you a sense of purpose. Below are some goals that you might choose for yourself:

- Complete a course of study, as a qualification to use, or for interest only.
- Learn a language.
- Learn to play a musical instrument.
- Join a band or choir.
- Learn to draw or paint, or do pottery.
- Increase your fitness and lose weight.

- Take on an allotment.
- Become a local councillor.
- Move to another part of the country, or abroad.
- Travel to far-off places.
- Learn to fly.

You can probably think of others. It does not matter if you change your mind, or abandon them in due course. What is important is that each goal gives you a sense of purpose, a sense of future and something to work towards.

Make New Social Contacts

Human beings are essentially social animals, and it is a rare person indeed who does not feel the need for some social contact, however minimal. Work gives people a ready-made social group, and a sense of belonging. There tend to be three levels of social contact, and different people value different types. The most outgoing people revel in meeting as many new people as possible, others are happy with one or two close friends or family members, while a middle group have a selection of friends that they tend to stick to. Retirement may provide an opportunity to spend more time with family members, and this can be hugely rewarding, or highly stressful, depending on the nature of your relationships with them. Sometimes you may want or need to take on a caring or helping role for a family member. We shall look more closely at these issues in chapter six. However, in the meantime, here are some ideas for replacing the social contacts that you have lost from work:

- Become a volunteer for a charity or group that helps others.
- Teach a course at your local adult education centre.
- Work in a charity shop.
- Work voluntarily for a national organization such as the National Trust.
- Volunteer to work at a local tourist attraction.
- Join a new club or sports team.
- Take up a new hobby or course of study.
- Become involved in local affairs.
- Become a school governor.
- Arrange to meet regularly with your existing friends.
- Plan regular visits with family members that you don't see every day.

Once again, this list is not exhaustive, but may give you some ideas. At the very least, try and ensure that you get out and see other people at least once a week. If you live alone, then you may want to have more contact than this.

Refer back to your picture of what kind of person you are, and try to plan your social calendar accordingly. You may want to include some social activity every day, or you may be the kind of person who is happy with much less. It may not be a good idea to rely solely on your partner for company, if you have one, as this can put a strain on your relationship.

Volunteering in Retirement

One of the most obvious ways to replace what used to be provided by work is to volunteer. Most volunteer positions require that you make a commitment to a certain number of hours, probably on particular days, and this will give a regular shape to your week, which you may find helpful.

You can work with those who are older and infirm, children, those with disabilities, people with mental health problems, animals, communities, museums, political groups (local and national), the criminal justice system and charities. You can work indoors or outside. You can do everything from writing letters to working in a shop. You may be a guide to a local attraction, or a book-keeper. You might be making tea, or driving people who cannot drive themselves to a doctor's or hospital appointment. You might even be involved in an archaeological dig, or cataloguing items in your local museum.

Before you rush into volunteering, however, do bear in mind that most organizations require a definite commitment from you, just as an employer would. You cannot just turn up when you feel like it. Indeed, some will want to interview you, and may even ask for references. If you work with children or vulnerable people, there may be a need for police security checks too. In effect you may be taking on many of the responsibilities of a paid job, without the money. Be sure that what you get back from your volunteering role is going to be worth what you have to put in, in terms of commitment.

Make sure also that you won't be out of pocket. Travelling can be expensive, and many places now charge for parking. There may be meals to pay for, and you may even need special clothing. Volunteering can be great fun, and is a marvellous way of restoring many of the things that retirement may have removed from your life, but it can be a big commitment to take on, especially if you are going to give several days of your week to it. Know your limits, and do not be afraid to say no if you feel you are being asked to do too much. Start small, until you know what is involved. You can always do more, but once committed it may feel more difficult to pull out.

If what you miss most is the feeling that you are doing something useful and/or important, volunteering may be just what you need to fill that gap. Local libraries, once again, will have information about a range of local groups, and if you have access to the internet, a quick search will soon find you dozens of local and national opportunities. Local papers may also have information about local groups and their events, where you will have the chance to meet others and discuss what is available. Local schools and residential homes for the elderly or for those with disabilities may also welcome volunteers. If you don't feel brave enough to ring them, perhaps you could write and offer your services.

Developing Existing Roles

All of us have some roles that we do not lose when we retire. We may be a partner or spouse, parent, child, niece or nephew, grandparent and neighbour. In addition to adding new roles to replace the ones lost from work, there may be a lot of satisfaction in developing existing roles, even if you are not taking on a role as a carer.

You may also have existing roles within the local community which you can also develop further. Retired people often play a significant role within their local community because they have the time to devote to the necessary activities which those who are still working cannot afford. If you are already involved in these to some extent, now may be a good time to see what else you can offer.

A New You

It is easy to see, therefore, that although you will lose some roles through giving up your current job, there are many ways of acquiring new ones. This might be through other ways of earning money, or by volunteering. It could also be by becoming more involved in community activities, sports or education. To a large extent, the world is your oyster, and you are likely to have a freedom of choice that is greater than at any time since you left school. Of course, limited money or poor health may slow you down a little, but the biggest obstacle to change and progress is likely to be the way you think about yourself, your future and your age. Confront your attitudes to age and retirement, and challenge any thoughts that make you feel hopeless. You can really make some significant changes in your life if you decide that is what you want to do.

4

Coping With Change

While old age and retirement inevitably bring changes, it is becoming clear that the way in which older people are managing their retirement and old age is also changing. Interestingly, it has been found in some surveys that many people in the sixty-five to seventy-five age group still describe themselves as 'middle-aged' rather than 'elderly' or 'old'.

Many people like the idea of retiring in their fifties, but have not really thought through the implications. Very often what they actually want to do is retire from their current job, and do something different. In addition, for the last few years investments have performed poorly, and many feel concerned that their pension plans will not provide for them in the way that they had hoped. The increase in the number of elderly people in society is likely to mean that many more people have to keep working because they, and society, will not be able to afford for them to stop. This means that retirement in the old sense may become increasingly difficult to achieve. More and more of us may have to accept that we need to do some paid work in order to survive.

Current changes in the world of work also mean that people will change jobs, retrain and take new directions much more frequently than in the past. This is now true for older workers as well as the younger ones, and many 'retired' people are simply changing the nature of their work, working fewer hours or becoming self-employed. Retirement inevitably brings changes, although they may be different from those experienced by previous generations.

Change is a Challenge

Change is always a challenge to our coping abilities, and the bigger the change, the harder it will be to adapt. Most people like to establish little routines for themselves, and the longer we stay in one place or one set of routines, the more we resent our comfortable lives being disturbed. Change can produce anxiety and fear, especially when previous experience of change has not been good. Some people cope with change by trying to ignore or deny it. Others, however, find change easier to cope with, and may relish plenty of variety and regular new challenges. Most of us, however, tend to like things to stay reasonably constant and predictable. It makes us feel safe. Some people start out enjoying change and variety, but as they get older, they begin to value stability more. Retirement is going to change your life, and for many people, everything changes at once: money, home life, relationships, place, routine, travelling and the level of intellectual stimulation available. No wonder it can be stressful!

Coping with change is almost never easy. It can be exciting, but it can also feel threatening. When you retire, it will inevitably take time to re-establish a way of life which feels comfortable and meets your needs. However, don't forget that change can also lead to growth, even if it is painful.

For those whose retirement has been forced upon them, whether by ill health, redundancy or an inflexible employer, the process of adapting to change can be much more difficult. In these circumstances, it is easy to feel that you have been dumped, like so much rubbish, with a resulting sense of uselessness and even despair. However, don't give up. There is hope.

Even when people have chosen to retire, they often do so simply because they have reached the appointed age of sixty or sixty-five, and it appears to be expected of them. This does not mean that they have planned their future, and when they suddenly find themselves at home all day with nothing to do, they can feel completely set adrift.

Stages of Adaptation

There have been a number of studies over the years that have looked at how people cope with life changes. Where the change is an unwanted one, as above, or with bereavement, for example, people typically react at first with numbness or disbelief. This is then followed by feelings of distress as they begin to acknowledge their loss, followed by anger, and later despair. Ultimately these feelings will be followed by acceptance, and then reorganization, as the person moves on to the next stage of life.

Individuals vary a great deal in how well or quickly they move through these phases. Moreover, the phases may come and go, so that the person does not necessarily move cleanly from one to the other, but perhaps moves backwards and forwards between the stages before eventually completing the process. Although the above stages were originally defined in terms of bereavement, when people have had a life change thrust upon them, such as compulsory retirement or redundancy, one can often see a very similar process in action.

Usually four stages of adaptation can be identified:

- Relinquishing (accepting the loss or change).
- Recess (a period of rest and recuperation).
- Redefinition (what next?).
- Re-engaging (moving forward again).

It is worth noting that even when a change is positive, there is still a need for this process, which enables the person to move from one stage of life to another. A period of 'recess' (rest and recuperation) is seen as a necessary stage, and this might correspond to the period where the retired person begins by having an extended break or holiday before making new plans.

Occasionally, people do find it extremely difficult to complete a process of adaptation, and seem to get stuck at one phase. Often this will be the result of earlier experiences, where a loss has not been properly dealt with, and there is unfinished business. An imposed change can also leave the person feeling like a victim, and if there have been earlier experiences of victimization, this can resurrect all kinds of difficulties.

For those who have been victimized in early life (for example, by being abused as a child or severely bullied at school), the issue of control is central. As soon as they are placed in a position where they feel that control has been lost, they will feel frightened and powerless again. If this is true of you, it may be useful to seek professional help. Such experiences can be difficult to deal with alone.

Life Events

The transitions that take place as we grow up – from baby to child, from child to adult, from school pupil to student, and from single person to being part of a couple – all bring significant changes. Each requires a process of adaptation. In recent years, we have come to refer to these changes as 'life events'. There has been considerable research into the effects of life events, and since the 1960s it has been well known that major events, such as bereavement, divorce or being made redundant, can have significant effects on both physical and mental health. As well as dealing with the psychological stages of adaptation, people are more likely to become physically ill after experiencing one of these major negative life events than at other, less stressful times. The illness may be as slight as getting a cold, or as serious as a heart attack.

What is perhaps less widely recognized is that even positive life events are stressful and that becoming engaged, getting married, becoming a parent and even moving to a new house can all cause the same kinds of problems of adaptation as the more negative kinds of events already described. Any change will have both positive and negative elements, and these will require the person who is going through the change to adapt and to respond differently. The experience of retirement, whether you are pleased or not about it, will also require you to adapt, and this process of adaptation is always stressful to some degree.

Find a pen and paper, and think back to all the major changes that have occurred in your life. Examples might be getting married, getting divorced, losing a parent, becoming a new parent for the first time, moving to a new part of the country, living away from home for the first time, and so on. Each person's list will, of course, be a bit different, but try and think of at least two or three of your own major life changes.

Now make two columns, headed 'Gains' and 'Losses', and list those that followed from each major life event that you have recalled. The balance of gains against losses will probably determine whether the change felt like a good one, or a bad one. Sometimes the balance may be about equal, but perhaps in addition, something good came out of the change in the long run, even though it wasn't immediately obvious that it would. An example of this might be being made redundant from a job you didn't really like. Although being made redundant is not usually a pleasant process, it may be that you received a lump sum in redundancy pay that enabled you to set up your own business, or pay off your mortgage, so that ultimately you were in a much better position. Sometimes what feels like a disaster at the time turns out to have unexpected benefits.

Sometimes a busy working life has offered a way of avoiding the confrontation of some difficult personal issues. These might be problems with your close relationships, difficulties arising from past trauma or generally poor self-esteem. When the role, identity and structure provided by work are removed, the newly retired person can suddenly find they feel exceptionally vulnerable and anxious. If you find yourself in this situation, it may be helpful to talk to your doctor, and perhaps seek some counselling or therapy.

Managing the Change

It seems clear, then, that change is stressful and will bring both gains and losses. Sudden, major change is always more difficult to handle than gradual, slower change. Many companies now offer the chance to retire gradually. This means that you can reduce your hours or days bit by bit, until you either retire completely, or you remain on a part-time contract indefinitely. This can be an excellent way to manage the changes that retirement brings. You can gradually detach yourself from the workplace and from colleagues, and equally gradually you can build up home- or community-based interests and activities to fill the spaces left by work. If your bosses are happy with this arrangement, it can offer one of the easiest routes into retirement. Even if ill health is forcing you into retirement, you may be able to plan a gradual withdrawal, which will make it easier to adapt.

Unfortunately, some employers are still pretty inflexible about retirement, and if yours is one of these, you may have no option but to go from full-time working to full-time retirement. This is a massive change, and it will take a while to get used to. Some people make it worse for themselves by denying that the reality of retirement is approaching, and so reach the final date almost completely unprepared for what lies ahead. This can result in both anxiety and depression when the reality hits home.

Understand How *You* Adapt to Change

Adapting to retirement will be much easier if you have a clear idea of how you cope with change generally. There is no doubt that some people cope much better than others, and some, as we noted earlier, actively seek variety. Think back over your life, and try and remember when you have experienced major changes in the past. How did you react? Did these changes seem frightening or threatening, or did they seem exciting? Think back to your school days. How did you react to changes of class, or school? (Maybe you can't remember. If your parents are still alive, you might ask them, or perhaps a brother or sister will remember.)

Look back at your list of your major life events. In addition to noting losses and gains, can you also recall how you actually felt? Was it easy to adapt? How long was it before these changes felt comfortable? It may be hard to remember, but it is an exercise which can help you to know yourself better.

Here is a further list of possible life events that might be relevant, in addition to those already considered. See how the list compares with yours. It does not matter if yours are different. Once again, try to remember how you felt at the time.

- Starting school
- Going to secondary school
- Your first job
- Your first serious relationship
- Getting married, or moving in together
- Becoming a parent
- Moving to a new job
- A major promotion
- Buying a house
- Moving to a different area or part of the country
- Facing a major reorganization of your workplace
- Losing a parent or family member
- Being made redundant

You may not have experienced all of these, but if you can recall five or six events that were important to you, you should begin to see some kind of pattern emerging. Were you excited by change? Did you go into each new experience expecting that you would be able to cope, or did you feel overwhelmed? Did you feel scared? Did it affect your ability to sleep or eat? Was your mental or physical health affected? Looking back do you focus on the positive things about the experience, or the negative ones? Which are the changes that you found most difficult?

This exercise should add to your picture of what to expect from yourself when you face the challenge of retirement. Try to be brutally honest with yourself. Don't give the answers that you feel you should. For example, you may feel that when your father died you should have grieved a lot for him, when actually your relationship was so difficult that a large part of your feeling was relief. There is nothing wicked in acknowledging these feelings. They are simply part of you.

You may find this exercise painful to do, but it can be very useful in helping you to understand how you might react to retirement. If you have already retired, it may help to explain why you feel the way you do. Think also about how you coped with your feelings in the past, when faced with these earlier life changes. Did you talk to others, and if so, who? Are you someone who bottles things up? What helps you most, when faced with difficulties? If you can recognize what helps you cope, you can try and include that in your plan too.

It is important to accept that part of the normal process of adjusting to change will be a period of grieving for what has been lost. It is quite normal to feel sad about the loss of money, status, professional identity or work colleagues, or indeed all of these. What is important is to try and ensure that you do not get stuck in this process of grieving and thus fail to be able to move on and take advantage of your next stage of life.

Active Adaptation

Having looked at how you coped in the past, you should now be beginning to see how you might react to the challenge of retirement. Your goal will be to set up a process of active adaptation, which will allow you to move through the process of change more easily. If you are struggling, it may be worth considering getting professional support for a while. If that doesn't appeal, or if you feel you cannot afford it, try keeping a detailed diary of your thoughts and feelings at this time. This can be enormously helpful in clarifying how you are reacting to the process of retirement. Writing down your thoughts is a way of making them more objective, and it can help you to identify themes that recur, which probably reflect what is really important to you. You don't need to show these to anyone else, and once you feel you have come through to the other side, you can always burn your diary, if you want to!

There are several ways in which people adapt to retirement, and there is no right or wrong way. The yardstick is whether you are happy with the choices that you have made. If you are unhappy, then it suggests that something still needs to change.

Some people, especially those who have been in managerial roles, can have trouble letting go of the idea that they are still somehow responsible for something, and for those whose career has been everything to them, it may be a real struggle to adapt. The bigger your losses, the harder it will be to fill the gaps they leave. Adapting to retirement may well prove to be as big a challenge as anything you faced at work. Are you ready for it?

Look After Yourself

We have noted how stressful change can be, but the process of adaptation will be easier if you take steps to manage the stress that you are experiencing. Stress management is a huge area, but the following ideas should help you to look after yourself more effectively as you work through the process of change.

Learn to Relax

This doesn't mean slumping in front of the telly and doing nothing. Real relaxation requires paying attention to your body. The simplest way is to get hold of a pre-recorded relaxation tape or CD, which will guide you through the process, step by step, until you achieve a state of deep relaxation. You can get such tapes or CDs from health food shops, or buy them online. Try to relax fully at least once a day. We shall look at relaxation in more detail in the chapter on health.

Make Sure That Your Life Has a Range of Different Activities

There is a lot of talk these days about a 'work/life balance', although many people in Britain still work ridiculously long hours and feel that they need to be on call permanently. In retirement you are freed from the demands of work but you still need to ensure that your life contains a balanced range of activities and interests.

Get Some Regular Exercise

We have already mentioned the importance of exercise generally, but in addition to maintaining your health, it can be invaluable in helping you to reduce your stress levels. Anxiety produces an increase in stress hormones such as adrenaline, and exercise can burn this up and help you to relax better afterwards. If you don't do anything else, then get out and walk for half an hour each day. Go and buy a paper from the local shop, walk the dog or just wander around the local park. Other good, easy exercise routines include regular gardening and housework – yes, housework. Scrubbing a floor, or heaving a vacuum cleaner up and down stairs is good aerobic exercise, and useful too. These all have the advantage of being free. You don't need to do a lot of exercise – twenty minutes to half an hour a day is all you need to keep your body fit – but it does need to raise your heart rate, and breathing rate too, if it is to do any good.

Make Time for Home and Family

When you work long hours, it is easy to forget that you are working to make a home for you and your family. Now you are retired, make a point of planning times to spend together. Good relationships will blossom, and poorer ones can often be improved by a little more attention. The emotional benefits will be good for you and your family members. Take time to create and maintain a pleasing environment for you and your family. This does not necessarily mean spending lots of money. Take time to declutter, clean and tidy your surroundings; this can have a huge impact on how you feel.

Examine Your Thoughts

The way you think about yourself and your life affects how you feel. There are many occasions when the way that we think about a situation can cause us a great deal of distress. Cognitive behavioural therapy, or CBT, can help you manage the process of change that retirement brings. There has been a huge interest in this approach in recent years, and it is now seen as the most important and useful tool available for helping those who are suffering from a range of mental disorders. While it has its limitations, this kind of therapy can be immensely helpful in dealing with many psychological difficulties.

CBT has two parts. The process of challenging your automatic thoughts is the cognitive part. Cognitive just means something to do with thinking, and how the brain uses information. The behavioural part is about what you do, including trying out new things. Often by experimenting with new activities or patterns of behaviour, you can help yourself to challenge your negative programming. In essence, it aims to help you examine and change the way you think about what happens to you. A change of perspective can make things much easier to manage, and greatly reduce the distress experienced. It has been said that it is not what happens to you that is important, but it is how you think about it. CBT aims to help you change the way you think about things.

The way we think about the world develops from our early experiences. If you grew up in a family that was supportive, helpful and positive towards you, then you are much more likely to grow into an adult who is confident and friendly, and expects largely good things from the world. You will probably find it relatively easy to make friends, and are less likely to see change as threatening. If, on the other hand, you grew up in a family that was abusive, unhelpful or highly critical of you, then you are more likely to grow into an adult who is uncertain, anxious and expects the worst from the world in general. Early learning experiences teach us what to expect from others, and shape how we think about ourselves. Negative early experiences are unhelpful and more likely to result in psychological problems in later life. Positive ones are more often associated with good mental health in later life.

However, other factors also affect how we are as adults. People do seem to be born with different types of responses to the world. Some people are naturally more anxious, especially when faced with novelty. Some are more adventurous and outgoing. Some are placid and easily pleased; some are more demanding and active. These differences can be seen from very early life onwards, and are probably unchangeable.

The combination of biological characteristics and early experience determine what kind of adult we become. By the time we reach retirement age, these habits of thinking and being will be deeply ingrained, and not easy to change. However, CBT can help. While it is not possible to change your underlying nature, or to change your early life experiences, with practice you can change how you react to difficulties. It is not what happens to you, but how you think about it, that matters.

Becoming Aware of Your Programming

Some people will find these exercises easier than others. Some will be more naturally tuned in to what is going on in their heads, and be able to describe this more readily. If you find this difficult, then begin simply by labelling your feelings as 'good' or 'bad', without worrying too much about more detail at this stage. Sit down in a quiet place, where you will not be disturbed, and try to become aware of your thoughts in relation to retirement. Write these down. If you have not yet retired, try and imagine how you will feel when you do. Will your retirement day be a good day or not? Probably there will be a mixture of good and bad feelings. What kinds of thoughts go with these feelings?

For example, retirement may result in the following kinds of thoughts going through your mind:

- 'Well, that's the end of me then.'
- 'What on earth will I do with myself?'
- 'I really don't know how I'll manage on a pension.'
- 'I don't want to be a pensioner.'
- 'I'm too young to retire.'
- 'I feel as if I am being put on the rubbish heap.'
- 'Now it is just a long road to death.'
- 'I'm going to miss all this.'
- 'I feel that I am useless.'
- 'This is not fair, I am not ready for this.'

You can see that negative thoughts like this will not make you feel good emotionally. They are likely to make you feel depressed, anxious or angry, or all three. This is the essence of CBT – *your thoughts lead to your emotions*. In other words, what you think determines what you feel.

Now look at this list. These might be the thoughts of someone who is looking forward to retirement:

- 'Great! No more getting up early.'
- 'Free at last!'
- 'I am really looking forward to being able to do what I want.'
- 'It will be so good to get away from all the office politics.'
- 'I shall really enjoy having more time to see my friends and family.'
- 'It will be great to have the time to sort out the house/garden.'
- 'I will enjoy the chance to do something completely different.'
- 'I could join an evening class.'
- 'I'm going to learn to play a musical instrument.'
- 'Thank goodness! No more bossy bosses.'

How differently the person with these kinds of thoughts is likely to feel from the one with all the negative thoughts!

Where do these thoughts come from? Probably you will say that they just pop into your head. We call these your 'automatic thoughts'. You don't plan or organize them – they just seem to turn up. These automatic thoughts are the result of your life experiences. If your early life experiences have led you to mistrust or fear the world in general, your automatic thoughts are more likely to be negative ones. We also know that people who are depressed have more negative automatic thoughts than people who are not. Unhappy experiences seem to predispose you to have negative automatic thoughts, and these negative thoughts tend to keep you feeling bad.

Worse still, other studies have shown that we tend to look at the world through distorting glasses. We see only those bits of it that support our automatic thoughts.

For example, people who fear failure may have automatic thoughts like 'I shall never be able to do this', 'Everything I do goes wrong' or 'I am useless at this'. Thoughts like these do not engender confidence, and thus the person is likely to fail again, thus confirming their opinion of themselves as a failure. Bizarrely, they also tend to ignore those times when things do go well, assuming that this is just a fluke, and nothing to do with them. Good experiences don't change the underlying view that they have of themselves as a failure.

Other people, like the person with the positive thoughts above, have distorting glasses of a different and more helpful kind. Their thoughts will be along the lines of 'I know I can do this, I have done it before', 'I know I am good at this', 'I enjoy a new challenge' or 'If it goes wrong, I'll just have to try something else'. This means that they approach any new challenge with confidence, and are much more likely to succeed. They also are much more likely to believe that a failure is nothing to do with them but just an accident, or the result of an experiment, from which they can learn something useful.

If you are prone to negative thoughts, can you do anything about it? Well, you can, and this is where CBT can help. You can begin to work on changing the negative thoughts to positive ones right away.

Changing Your Automatic Thoughts

Changing your thoughts is not easy, and it takes some work, but it can be done. The first step is to become aware of your automatic thoughts. Write down any thoughts that pop into your head when you think about being retired and your future life. For most people these automatic thoughts will not necessarily be all negative (bad) or all positive (good). They will be a mixture of both. That does not matter. The important part at this stage is to get used to identifying them. Your diary may be helpful here – you will notice if certain thoughts or feelings keep recurring.

The next stage is to look at what feelings are associated with these thoughts. Does a particular thought make you feel angry, anxious, depressed, helpless or just plain bad? These feelings can be powerful, and it is not enough just to say 'that's nonsense' and try to ignore them. However, what you can do is question the thinking that leads to those thoughts. You need to try and take off those distorting glasses and ask yourself: 'What evidence do I have that my view is the right one?'

Let's suppose that your overwhelming automatic thought about retirement is: 'Well, my life is over now.' What makes you think that? Is it perhaps because your father died soon after retirement? Or maybe you have friends who did? How likely is it that you will follow the same pattern? Even if you are the image of your father, and like him in every way, you are not identical, and it is not certain that your life will mirror his. Has your life so far mirrored his? If not, why should it do so now? What other evidence have you got that leads you to believe that you will die soon after retirement? Is your health bad? Is your environment unhealthy?

Let us, for a moment, suppose the worst. You retire at sixty-five, and know that you probably only have two or three years of life left, for whatever reason. What would you do? Would you sit down in a chair or retire to bed for that remaining time? More likely you would decide to make the most of your last few years. You would perhaps plan the trip of a lifetime. You might have people that you would want to visit, perhaps people you have not seen for years. You might want to take up a new hobby while you still could. So what is the difference? You may have a year, five years, ten years or thirty. However much of life you have left, you can still plan to do those things that you really value.

This questioning process is called *challenging* your automatic thoughts. That does not mean saying they are nonsense. What it means is that you are actively seeking evidence to check out whether these thoughts are true or not. While some people may retire, give up and die quickly, there are many others who do not. To a great extent, you have choice. Even if you have a terminal illness, you can still choose to make the best of the time you have left.

However, remember that the initials CBT also include a 'B' for behaviour. It is important not just to change what you think, but also what you do. By changing your behaviour, you will change your experiences, your thinking, and thus your feelings. This is the real challenge, because your previous programming, and your automatic thoughts arising from that, will have convinced you that nothing can change. You need now to adopt an experimental approach, and just try something new. At the same time, you need to monitor what *really* happens, not what you automatically expect to happen. You may be surprised.

You may need to carry out a number of experiments before you become convinced that your thoughts have been incorrect. One positive experience can be dismissed as a lucky chance or a fluke, but if you have a series of good outcomes it is harder to ignore the evidence. Try to cultivate an open mind. Believe in yourself and your ability to adapt and change!

5

Managing Time and Solving Problems

Many of us are used to having to manage our time at work. Indeed, many employers provide training in time management for their employees. It may seem odd to think about managing your time at home, when in the past there has often been all too little of it. While it can be a joy to be freed from the tyranny of the clock, it can also feel like being set adrift in a rudderless boat. This chapter looks at how one can establish a new structure in life, without returning to the slavery to the clock which working often entails.

Once you have retired, nobody is setting clear goals for you, and the days may just seem to drift by. This can be a particular problem if you live alone, or if your partner is still working. If you are finding this a problem, or think that you will, then the obvious thing to do is set up your own timetable or structure. Some people do this easily, while others seem to struggle. However, it is possible to organize your retired life so that there is a structure, with some clear goals to work towards. This will help to give you a sense of achievement, rather than feeling that you are just drifting along.

When you first retire, there may be jobs around the house or in the garden that need doing. Write them all down, and assess roughly how long each will take. Do you have the necessary cash to proceed, assuming that cash is needed? If not, then prioritize. Decide what really needs doing and leave the rest, or look at other ways of doing things.

For example, if you need new curtains, can you make them yourself, or get some from a charity shop or second-hand curtain supplier? You now have plenty of time to look around for exactly what you want. Being retired means that you have not always got to take the shortest, quickest or easiest route to getting what you want. You have time to research things, shop around or make them yourself.

Once you have decided what your priority tasks are, then you could try laying out a timetable for yourself. Draw out the days of the week and look at how you might allocate the things you need to do to the different days. It may be a good idea to leave the weekends free, so that you can spend time with your partner or just mark these as different from the weekdays, in the same way as they were when you were at work. Do not attempt to fill every day completely, because there will always be some unexpected things that crop up. Try not to be too rigid. Part of the fun of retirement is that you can do things on the spur of the moment if opportunities arise.

If you find your timetable is not working very well, you can always change it. If you find you hate it, then abandon it! Remember that you are now in charge, and can do things your way. Nevertheless, if you are not good at organizing yourself, you may find that this is an effective way to get things done.

If you have the task of being the housekeeper, then it pays to take a similar approach to keeping house. Housework is notorious for filling whatever time is available. By setting out a timetable for regular and essential jobs, you can keep it under control, but still ensure that some days, or parts of days, are allocated to what you really want to do. If you find it hard to motivate yourself to do the routine jobs, then allocate a time slot to each essential job, and when it is complete reward yourself with something pleasant. That way you always have a pay-off for completing the tedious chores.

If you find it really difficult to organize yourself in this way, it may help to enlist the assistance of someone else in doing this. They can help you draw up a realistic timetable, and encourage you to stick to it. However, there is no point in doing this if it becomes a psychological battleground. If you do everything you can to avoid what is suggested, then you are both wasting your time. You have got to be committed to making it work.

Taking on a regular commitment of volunteering can help, as most organizers will want you to be available on particular days or at particular times. This can be an excellent way of getting others to help organize you. Or, if you decide to take on another job, full- or part-time, to take the place of the old one, this will give you the required structure. Alternatively, you could commit yourself to several regular outside activities, such as courses of study, or sports sessions, so you have a range of goals to meet. Once again you need to know yourself. What is most likely to work best for you, and what are you most likely to enjoy? Many people have a sport or hobby that they love, and once they retire are able to devote a great deal more time to it. Others find that they enjoy spending more time with family members. Offering to spend one day a week with someone that you care about can help both of you, as long as they are as keen as you are to set this up.

However, spending time with your spouse or partner is something that will need particular attention. If you neglect each other your relationship will almost certainly begin to suffer. On the other hand, if you spend every minute of every day together you will soon find that you have little to say to each other, and one or both of you may begin to feel stifled. Some couples do manage to do this and remain content with each other, but most people find their relationship benefits if they spend some time apart. When deciding on your timetable, it is a good idea to make sure that you have some shared activities, but also some that you can do independently.

Back to Those Five Requirements

Do you remember those five requirements for a good retirement from chapter one? To remind you again, these were:

- Social contacts
- Physical activity

- Intellectual activity
- Creative activity
- A passion

Our aim is to try to include each of these in your final plan. If structure is something that you feel you need, then think about how you might structure your day or week to include all of these. Here is an example that might work:

Monday: Take my elderly mum to do her shopping and have lunch with her (social).

Tuesday: Attend a keep-fit class at the local sports centre, and then have a swim (physical).

Wednesday: Attend my French class in the morning, and then complete my homework for this in the afternoon (intellectual).

Thursday: Spend the day painting in watercolours, and framing some that I have already done (creative).

Friday: Spend the day in my garden, weeding, planting and planning (my passion).

This kind of timetable is not rigid, and could easily be changed or adapted if necessary, but it provides a framework which gives the week some structure, while fulfilling the five requirements that are listed above. Some activities will, of course, fulfil more than one of these. The sports and educational activities are likely to offer additional social opportunities, for example.

The problem with this kind of timetable is that each of the five areas is confined to a single day of the week.

This may not be ideal. We know that to be really effective, exercise is best taken little and often. A walk of a mile or two every day will be better for your overall health than one ten-mile walk once a week. Similarly, intellectual exercise is probably better taken little and often.

One way around this is to set up a daily plan which includes a small amount of each. You might spend a little time each day doing a crossword, or in the case of language study you could practise your language skills for a short time each day. As older people find that they tend to be slower in acquiring new learning this is probably a better way to learn anyway. You could also try to include a walk in your daily routine, perhaps to the local shops, or to take out the dog if you have one. (Perhaps you could get one?) If you are a keen gardener you could allocate an hour or two each day to gardening. This is probably better for your back than spending a whole day in the garden as suggested above. So an alternative daily timetable could look something like this:

- Tidy the kitchen and put a load of washing in the washing machine.
- Walk to the local shops to collect a newspaper and any items of shopping needed.
- Spend half an hour doing the crossword, or practising French verbs.
- Meet a friend for lunch.
- Spend a couple of hours in the garden, weeding and tidying.

Of course, not every day could or should be identical, but you can see that by breaking up the day you will have more variety and will not tend to exhaust yourself by doing too much of any one thing. Visiting your elderly mother, for example, may still need to take up most of a day, especially if she lives some distance away, but this could be balanced by the variety of the other days.

If your retirement plan is going to include more adventurous activities, such as rock-climbing or flying, then you will need to fit your other activities around the opportunities that you have to do these. You probably won't want or be able to do them every day, or even every week. By contrast, walking is an easy form of exercise, and can be done anywhere, although walking to the shops in the middle of a busy city may not be particularly pleasant or relaxing. You may find it better to do something that is more enjoyable, even if you can't do it every day.

You may find that one kind of timetable suits you better than another. Some activities will work for some people and not others. Experiment, and see which works best for you. There is no right or wrong here. The principles so far discussed are only a guide, and there is no point in setting yourself a timetable that becomes as much a source of stress as your working life was. Others dislike planning their days in this way, and are much happier to just drift along and do whatever takes their fancy. The best measures of a successful adaptation to retirement are your physical health and your happiness. If you are fit and content with your life, then you are probably doing fine.

Setting Goals

Anything that really interests you will usually get you involved in setting yourself goals. These may be competitive goals (for example, 'to be the best') or they may be personal goals (such as 'to be able to speak some basic French by the time we go to France next summer'). The goals will change, of course, and in the case of gardening, for example, you may find that you are constantly setting yourself new goals in the form of new projects: 'I am going to turn that bed into a rose garden' or 'This year I am going to try growing yellow tomatoes'.

Goals are important because they give us a sense of achievement and progress. If we have no goals we tend to drift along without direction. If we have too many goals we can get very stressed. The beauty of a retired life is that you can choose your goals, usually without interference from others. You can change them and abandon them if you decide they are not right for you. There is no one telling you what you must do, except perhaps your partner, who may want you to paint the house or reorganize the garden!

In setting your goals you probably need to reflect on the ideas discussed previously and think about your dreams, as well as the more practical demands of everyday life. There is no harm in having down-to-earth goals such as getting the house painted, but it is probably good for your soul to have some that are more exciting too. When you first retire, those goals may be just a list of outstanding jobs around the house, but as time goes by, and you work your way through these, it may be a good idea to spend some time thinking of your longer-term goals and how you might begin to work towards them.

Sometimes you may have a dream that you really decide is just beyond you. Either the money that is required is far too much, or your physical health is no longer up to it. Before you relinquish your goal completely, investigate whether you might be able to get part of the way there. You may not, for example, be fit enough to do a parachute jump unaided, but you may be able to do a jump in tandem with someone more experienced.

Getting More Done

For some people, the very freedom of retirement can be a problem. These are often the people who like to have structure in their lives. These folks often find that they drift from one task to another, perhaps not finishing anything very satisfactorily. This can be very frustrating and unsatisfying. If this sounds like you, then a timetable such as we have discussed can be enormously helpful. If you tend to switch on the TV in the morning and then find that you are still watching it at lunchtime, then maybe you need to take yourself in hand. When you were working, your working life limited the amount of time that you could spend watching TV, while now there are no such limits. Unless you want to spend the rest of your retirement watching TV, you need to act now!

You don't need to give up TV altogether, but put periods into your timetable when you will let yourself watch. This works best if you allow yourself a period of TV watching as a reward for having got another task done. You might decide you will only watch in the evenings, as another way of limiting it. The best solution for you will depend partly on how self-disciplined you can be. If you know that once you have switched the TV on, you will be drawn into watching one programme after another, then the best approach is to avoid switching it on at all until you have done something else that you need or want to do.

If you are slightly more disciplined, you might scan the TV listings for the day, and decide which programmes you really want to watch. You can then include these in your timetable and make sure that once your particular programme has ended you will turn off the TV and begin the next activity that is on your timetable. However, this takes more self-control, and some people simply find that it does not work for them.

Listening to the radio is less of a problem, because you can do this alongside many other activities, while TV watching tends to take most of your attention. If you spend a lot of time alone and like the company that TV seems to give, then try the radio as an alternative. Or try getting out more, and meeting some new friends.

Another approach, which is perhaps more challenging, but can be interesting to try, is to cultivate a Zen approach to the chores. Do them thoroughly and systematically, taking satisfaction from doing them as well as you can. If you have to scrub a floor, take pride in doing it as well as you can. If you need to clean the sitting room, do it thoroughly and carefully. This approach has a double benefit. By taking a pride in doing the activity well, you make it a positive activity, and you will begin to take pleasure in doing it. If it is done well and thoroughly it will need doing less often.

A Pattern or a Patchwork?

The beauty of working life is that the days and weeks have a pattern. Once you are retired, there is a danger that the days may develop a tedious sameness. We have discussed above the idea of having a day full of different activities, and this can work well for much of the time. However, it will do you good psychologically to break the pattern now and again. Plan the occasional day out for yourself, with or without your partner. This need not cost a lot of money. It is now possible in most areas of the UK to get free bus travel passes, which enable you as a pensioner to travel almost anywhere you like free of charge. Alternatively you could arrange a day out with friends that you don't often see, or to visit relatives who live some distance away.

In addition, there may be activities that only become available on a monthly basis (or even less frequently) that you wish to include in your plan. You might want to enrol for an occasional study day. These can cover anything from Tudor cookery to aromatherapy. Unusual extras like this will make a break in your weekly routine. Don't forget to plan some holidays, too. Depending on your financial situation these might range from a week in a caravan in Wales, to a trip down the Amazon. In any case, the break from regular routine is likely to do you good.

A generation or so ago, it was quite common for house-wives who were at home all the time to have a pattern to their week where, for example, they did the washing on Mondays, ironing on Tuesdays, cleaning on Wednesdays and Thursdays, and shopping on Fridays. It seems that as human beings we often like structure, and seek to impose it on ourselves, even when other people do not. However, part of the real joy of retirement is the freedom that it can bring, so make sure that you do not waste this rare gift. While a regular pattern can be helpful, do not allow it to take over your life, and be prepared to dump it temporarily if a new opportunity that really appeals comes along. At a psychological level it is not helpful to be ruled by 'musts' and 'oughts', whether these are imposed by others or by yourself. Work on giving yourself choices and a life that is perhaps a colourful but structured patchwork rather than a rigid pattern.

Demands from Others

Inevitably if your life is lived in close proximity to others they will impose demands on you from time to time. Often these will be no problem, and you will be happy to try and please those whom you love. However, it can happen that once you are retired you are seen as fair game by some less thoughtful friends or family members. Because you are at home all the time they may expect that you will do, for example, all the housework, all those jobs around the house that have been waiting for ages, endless child-minding and babysitting, or fetching and carrying for them. Sometimes, elderly parents can become unreasonably demanding, expecting that because you are now at home much more, you will be able to spend a lot more time with them and doing things for them.

This can be difficult to deal with, because on one level they are right. You do, indeed, have a lot more time to give and you may feel that you should do what you can. However, do bear in mind that you have had your time at work, when you coped with all the problems and demands that go with that, and it is now time for you to have a period of rest and recuperation. Elderly parents may have looked after and helped their parents, but that does not automatically mean that you are obliged to help yours.

Take some time to think about your own needs too. If you genuinely enjoy the company of your parents, children or grandchildren, then by all means give them as much time as you wish. You will all benefit. However, it may not be good for you to commit your whole life to them. You have the right to take some time out, to do what you want to do, on your own, and it will probably do you good to have a break. The very old and the very young can both be very wearing, and it may do your own health good to recognize this and build in some free time to your week or month. On the other hand, being needed by your family may help to give your life a sense of meaning and the structure that you are missing.

A more difficult situation may arise when you feel obliged to help out, but would really rather not. This may be because you have other goals and dreams that you want to follow, or it may be simply that you do not particularly enjoy the company of the family member who is asking for your time. People can be a joy to be with, or the complete opposite. Sometimes you may leave a visit with a sigh of relief to have got away. People who are difficult, demanding, tetchy or ungrateful can be very tiresome to spend time with, and there is no law that says you must. Do not be ruled by guilt or emotional blackmail. On the other hand, it may pay to ask yourself why the person is behaving in such a way. Such difficult people are often unhappy, anxious and lonely, and just not very good at getting what they need from others in a positive way. You will need to be firm but kind, if you are faced with such a situation. Make it clear that while you are willing to help, you also need to have your own life. However, reminding yourself from time to time of the possible reasons for the difficult behaviour may make it easier for you to cope with.

A Balancing Act

When you were working, you would often have to cope with a range of demands and expectations from others, and most people cope with these by dividing up their time so that they can do a bit of everything. The same principle applies to giving your time to the demands of others. If you genuinely want to help or enjoy helping your relative, then allocate a proportion of your day, week or month to them and then stick to that. Try not to let them bully you into giving more than you want to, or more than you feel they really need.

Similarly, try to balance the time you give to all your activities. The work/life balance is usually discussed in the context of the working life, but the same principles also apply in retirement. As organisms we are not built to do the same things over and over again. If sensory stimulation remains the same for a long time, we stop seeing, hearing or feeling it.

If required to watch out for something continuously as, for example, when scanning a radar screen for long periods to detect incoming aircraft, it has been known for many years that the watcher's arousal gradually drops to the point where they miss what they are actually looking for. When forced to do or watch or listen to the same things for long periods, we switch off and we get bored. If we have to make the same physical movements over and over again, joints, tendons and muscles complain; we develop RSI (repetitive strain injury) or bad backs, knees or ankles. Variety keeps us active and healthy so whatever else you do make sure that you build some variety into your new retired life.

Planning for the Longer Term

As we have noted more than once, the main change that has happened in relation to retirement is that the baby-boomer generation can expect, with luck and good health, to live for many more years after retirement. Women still tend to live a little longer than men, but both sexes can now expect to have a reasonable chance of reaching their eighties.

One of the most commonly expressed plans for retirement among the new generation of pensioners is that they will retire from their current occupation in their fifties, or early sixties, and then begin again in a completely new direction. While many of these people also comment that they do see themselves stopping work completely at some stage, they tend to put this off as something to happen some years after the conventional retirement age. They do not see themselves as ready to stop yet.

Interestingly, many prospective pensioners now reject both full-time work and full-time leisure. They have, it seems, taken to heart the message of work/life balance and see their ideal life as including some part-time work as well as time for new leisure activities, or increased participation in old ones. Some are keen to start their own business, or work from home, and this seems to reflect a wish to have more control over their lives, especially their working lives. Others think it likely that they will alternate between periods of leisure and periods of work, possibly financing the leisure activities with the periods of work. A relatively small proportion of pensioners seem to want to stop work completely and never work for money again.

What is particularly interesting is that although money is an issue for many, it is not necessarily the main consideration in making these decisions. The majority feel that it is the mental stimulation and challenge that work brings which keeps them in the game. Others value the social contacts that work brings, while some just like the structure. The main challenge of retirement is to find ways of restructuring your life so that it is even more satisfying than before.

Can You Get it Right?

From our earlier exercises you should now have gained some awareness of whether you are someone who prefers structure and predictability or not. In the course of looking at ways to structure time during your retirement, we have examined a number of ideas. It is important not to feel that you 'must' or 'should' follow any of these guidelines if you feel uncomfortable with them. As long as you are not harming others or breaking the law, you do not need to live your life by other people's rules.

My aim is to help you to become self-aware and to develop the skills necessary to make this next phase of your life a rewarding and satisfying one. The best yardstick for success, as already mentioned, is that you are content and happy with your life. The suggestions that aim to promote good health, while not necessarily the most welcome, are to ensure you have the maximum number of years possible to enjoy your new way of life. Nevertheless, you have choices, and one of those may be to continue to live your existing unhealthy life if you are genuinely happy with it. The most important question to ask yourself is 'Am I content with myself and my life?' If the answer is 'yes', then you are probably doing fine. Cultivate an awareness of your feelings. If you feel bad, then something needs attention. If you feel good, you have probably got things about right.

Problem-solving

Problem-solving is part of life. Life is full of problems, large and small, and we all develop a range of problem-solving skills as we move through life. The difficulty that many of us have, however, is that emotions get in the way of logical problem-solving and sometimes make it hard for us to see what is going on. Once we become seriously depressed, our assessment of our problems becomes distorted by emotion, and the picture that we paint for ourselves is clouded by a dark filter of unhappiness.

Most of us solve our problems in one of three ways. We either worry away at them on our own until we work out a solution, or we chew them over with anyone who will listen, until either we or they come up with an idea that seems a plausible solution. If neither of those approaches works then we tend to get stuck fretting and fuming about their insolubility. In the latter case, this can lead to distress and depression.

Some people use avoidance as a strategy. Faced with a problem, they ignore it for as long as they can, and either the problem goes away, or becomes so large that it can no longer be ignored. This can work to an extent, but it does mean that some small problems which could be nipped in the bud cause huge problems later on because they have been neglected. This is particularly true of health problems, which are almost always easier to solve if caught early.

The best strategy for problem-solving is ideally a more structured one. Most problems are complex, and it is this very complexity that makes them hard to solve. If you can analyse the problem logically, breaking it down into its various components, you can often work out a solution to each component part and thus overall to the big problem.

For example, if your problem is that you are bored and lonely at home after retirement this could be broken down into the following components:

- I have no friends nearby, and my partner is at work all day.
- I find it hard to make new friends, and I am quite shy.
- I am not good at organizing my time when I am alone.
- Since retiring I don't have much spare money.
- I miss feeling useful.

You then need to consider each part on its own. A solution to part one would be to make friends nearer home, or persuade your partner to retire, or both. A solution to part two would be to have an activity that brings you into contact with others, as your work used to do, so that you don't feel that you must go out and actively seek new friends. A solution to part three might be to find a volunteer role where you will have a timetable set for you by the organization, or to look for another job. A solution to part four would be to find an activity near to home which did not require much financial outlay, or to look for another job. A solution to part five would be to get involved in an activity that you felt was socially or practically useful. This could be another job, a volunteer role or a new role at home (taking over the shopping or housework, for example).

If you put all these together, there may be a good case for going back to some kind of paid work. Alternatively, you might enjoy taking on a voluntary role where you feel that what you are doing is socially useful and valuable. In both cases, something that brings you into contact with other people would be helpful. However, in view of your lack of money, this will have to be near home, and not incur any unnecessary extra expense for you. You then need to consider which of these options appeals most. Undoubtedly you will have more control over a volunteer role, in that you may have choices about what you do and when. On the other hand, you may feel that the lack of money is a big factor in stopping you enjoying life and so you feel that returning to work is the better option. You may wish to try both, and see which suits you better. Don't be afraid to experiment.

However, if you are feeling confused about which way to go, adopting this kind of structured problem-solving approach can help you to unravel what you really want. Writing things down, or drawing diagrams which help you to visualize your various options, can also help. Talking to someone else can also enable you to clarify your feelings and help you decide what you want. If you don't have friends or family who can assist in this way, and feel really stuck, think about seeing a counsellor.

6

Other People

As human beings we are essentially social animals. We have evolved to live in groups, and it is a rare person who does not feel the need for some kind of social contact. Most of us seem to prefer to live with at least one other person, although current demographics suggest that more and more people are living alone. This may have significant implications for their adjustment to retirement in the future.

Work provides a ready-made set of social contacts, and once you have retired, you lose this ready-made social environment. If you live alone, you may suddenly find that you are lonely. It is much easier to live alone if the bulk of your working week is spent among other people. However, if all of your days and evenings are spent alone, it is hardly surprising that you may start to feel somewhat isolated.

Even those who have a partner may find that they feel lonely. If your partner remains at work, while you retire, you will still spend many hours on your own unless you make plans to do otherwise. If you have both retired it may be less of a problem, but if your partner retired earlier, you may find that they have established their own life independently of you, and may even resent you suddenly expecting them to find time for you. This can lead to arguments and tensions. You therefore need to plan how you are going to make new social contacts and maintain the good ones that you already have.

Consider also if you are someone who enjoys meeting lots of new people on a regular basis. Think about your average day. How much time do you spend alone and how much with others? Are these others close family, friends or a much wider group of people? In which situation are you happiest? Do you feel that you need a bit of each to be completely happy, or are there some areas where you would be happier to lose these contacts?

Assessing Your Social Capital

Your social capital is the sum total of all the positive and helpful social contacts that you have. This will range from intimate contacts, such as partners and children, to other relatives, close friends, casual friends and acquaintances. You may also have social contacts that are restricted to certain areas of your life. These may be colleagues at work, people at a sports group or club, friends at a church and so on. You may only mix with these people in one setting, so that although you may know them quite well, they are not really close friends.

When you retire, your social capital will probably change or diminish. You will lose those people who were contacts at work, and you may need to plan actively to replace them. If your work was your life, you will be particularly vulnerable to this loss of social capital.

It may help to sit down and make a list of all those who contribute to your social capital. How often do you see each of them, and how often are you likely to continue to see them? Consider which people you value most, and with whom you would like to spend your time. Most of us have some acquaintances or even friends who have become habits rather than true friends, and this may be a good time to re-evaluate your relationship with them. You don't have to make a great issue of it, but you can quietly decide to let this or that relationship die. As one friend of mine used to say, friendships are like house plants – you need to go around and water them from time to time if they are to survive. At this point in your life there may be some that you will choose to let die.

On the other hand, there will probably be those whose company you value, and where you want to continue the friendship. If this friendship was work-based, you will need to plan when and how you are going to meet in the future. If they continue to work full-time after you have stopped, this may be difficult. Where you have other friends whom you value, you may now be able to see more of them. However, this probably won't happen unless you plan it.

Making New Friends

If your social capital seems limited, then you need to consider how you might remedy this. The ideal way is to join a group or activity that will enable you to meet new people. Ideally these will be people who, as well as being interesting, are geographically close. As you get older, and perhaps less fit, you may not want to travel long distances to maintain relationships, so it is a good plan to develop a local network of friends.

You may find these friends via a new job, or by starting a new activity such as a class. You might make new friends by going to the gym, or taking up a sport. Volunteering is also a good way to meet new people, both as potential friends and as casual acquaintances. However, it may take a while to develop new friendships, and you may need to make an effort to do so. If you are reserved and say little, it is unlikely that others will seek your company. To develop new friendships you need to show interest in other people, ask about their lives and interests, and spend time together. New activities and doing new things together can help to develop a friendship, because you are all in the same boat. Moving alone into an established group can be more difficult, but is not impossible.

Other local groups that may offer chances to make new contacts and friends are religious groups, political groups, charities or local attractions (especially if you are willing to volunteer to help). You might wish to consider joining a yoga or Pilates class, join a gym or start learning a new style of dance. You could join a cycling club or a rambling group. All these kinds of activities and groups can offer opportunities to find new social contacts.

It may be that you have ideas about activities that you would enjoy, but feel that you want to share them with someone else. Joining a class can be a good way to overcome this problem. Alternatively, you could ask around your existing friends and family to see who might like to join you. If that doesn't work, then you may need to be brave and just give it a try. There will often be others in the same boat, and this alone can be a basis for a friendship to develop.

If you are shy, you need to work at overcoming this, or you will make little progress. Almost everyone has times when they feel shy and you can often overcome these feelings by focusing on how others are feeling, rather than thinking about yourself. If shyness is a big problem for you, then maybe a therapist could help you with this. Your retirement plan also needs to include ways that you might meet others which feel less threatening. Perhaps a helping role might be a good way to make contact with others without undue pressure.

It is no use blaming others if you are lonely. People will not beat a path to your door unless you make some effort too. Many people will not make the first approach for fear of intruding. If you are feeling lonely, then perhaps you need to take that chance and make the first move. If it fails at least you will be no worse off than you are now!

Caring for Family Members

Most of us are fortunate enough to have a range of family contacts. These may be partners, parents, children, siblings, aunts and uncles or grandchildren, or indeed all of these. Inevitably we will value some of these people more than others. Just because you are related to someone does not mean that you will get on well together. However, if you have such contacts and are feeling lonely and isolated, it makes sense to seek out those who are closest to you first. You may find that you can improve and develop a relationship that has never been exceptional in the past just by giving it a little more time and attention.

Elderly parents, if they are still around, may be slow to ask for help because they are afraid of being a nuisance. However, if you make it known that you are available and willing to help, your offer may be received gratefully. You could find that you develop a new and closer relationship in their declining years, which will enrich life for all of you. Of course, some elderly parents can become demanding and difficult, or indeed may always have been so. In this case, you do not need to be unkind or rude, but simply be firm, and make it clear that you are happy to help, but will not give up your whole life to them. Of course, if you enjoy your parents' company, or are seriously concerned about their welfare, then you may choose to help out more often. If they are in need, or vulnerable, but you do not want to spend a lot of time with them, look at alternative ways of ensuring they have the help they need. Don't fall for emotional blackmail!

If a parent is sick or dying, then the situation is rather different, and you may feel that you must be there to help. However, being a carer in such a situation can be both demanding and draining, and you do need to take some time to look after yourself too. If you don't you will also become ill, and that won't help anyone. Ask your doctor about possible sources of help, and if necessary, do think seriously about nursing home care. It is never easy to place one's parent into such a home, but there are times when the task of nursing them is simply too much for one person to undertake, and that difficult decision will need to be made.

Sometimes it may be a partner who is unwell or dying. This can be particularly distressing, especially when you may have planned for a retirement period together, perhaps travelling or sharing a hobby. Unfortunately, the care-giving role often falls on older women, who end up caring for elderly parents or husbands, and sometimes even the husband's parents too. Women still tend to live longer than men, and they are more likely to become carers for their husbands than the reverse. Care-giving of this kind does not, of course, last forever, but it can be exhausting while it lasts. Don't be afraid to admit it if you are struggling. There is no shame in admitting that you need extra help in such a situation.

It may be that the caring you are called upon to do is not for the older members of the family, but the younger ones. These days, many young couples both have to work in order to afford to buy a house and maintain the standard of living that they want. The result of this is that many more grandmothers appear to be doing the caring for the next generation. There is perhaps no harm in this, as long as everyone is happy with this situation. However, if you are such a grandmother (or indeed grandfather) and find that you are being asked to do more caring than you would like, it is time to take a stand. You have done your share of parenting, and have worked hard throughout your life. You have raised your children, and they are now responsible for raising theirs – not you. Unless you are genuinely happy about taking over the care of your grandchild, or grandchildren, then make it very clear to your children what you are prepared to do, and what the limits are. Do not allow them to bully you, or take you for granted. You have probably spent much of your working life meeting the demands of other people. Retirement should be your time, and caring for young children is hard work. You need to be able to say 'no' if you want to. This is not selfish.

Of course, it may be that you dote on your grandchildren, and like nothing better than to spend time with them. If so, then that is fine. You will enjoy it, and they will benefit from the attention of an adult who is happy to give them as much as they want. For those who loved the role of being a parent, it may be a chance to relive one of the happiest periods of their life. However, do consider the fact that one day these grandchildren will also grow up, and stop needing you, and you may then need to have other strings to your bow.

Retirement and Partners

For most of us, a 'partner' still means a husband or wife, but if you are a gay couple the same issues will apply. There are three possible scenarios – one partner may retire while the other is still working, both may retire together, or one may retire to be at home when the other has been the main home-maker for some time. Each can present its own problems, and there are other issues that may arise too.

The first and most important thing to do when you are thinking about retirement is to discuss it with your partner.

This may seem obvious, but it is surprising how many people don't talk about the future. They plan day-to-day activities, weekends and holidays, but completely fail to acknowledge the possible impact of this huge life change which may be fast approaching. If one or both of you are going to retire within the next couple of years, start talking about it now.

Be honest with each other about what is really important to each of you. If, for example, a wife has gone back to work later in life, she may be reluctant to stop work when her husband does. Women of the baby-boomer generation may have had to fight hard for the right to work, and this may make it doubly difficult to decide to give it up. If that is the case, the woman needs to be honest about this, and the couple need to plan how the day-to-day tasks of running the house will be allocated, and how the husband may spend his time. It is clearly not a fair division of labour for the working wife to continue to have all the responsibilities of running the home, while her retired husband spends his days on the golf course.

Talk about money too. Not just about investments and pensions, but about how the money will be spent. Most people have less money after retirement than before, and there may be a need to change spending habits accordingly. People tend to fall into two camps – the spenders and the savers. If you are a spender, then you need to plan your budget carefully and allocate a fixed amount to spending, after which you must stop. If one of you is a spender and the other a saver, then this can be real a source of stress when income is reduced. If the one who retires is the spender, then this can also cause real problems. You need to be honest with each other about your spending patterns and about how you might regulate these in the future. Many women admit to hiding their expenditure from their husbands. This is likely to cause serious problems if money is tight. If your retirement is to go well, you need to sit down together now and plan a budget that will work as well as possible for both of you.

Previous studies have shown that where couples have successfully negotiated the problems that retirement can present, they are usually those who are best friends as well as partners, and are committed to their relationship. They are communicative with each other and have strategies to resolve problems. They have probably always had a good marriage and have learned how to negotiate the ups and downs of married life. Couples who adjust well to retirement are good at resolving conflict, and there is almost always some increase in marital conflict after retirement. Most couples argue or disagree from time to time. The relationships that survive are those in which the partners have learned to resolve conflict, not just avoid it.

Some studies in the past have suggested that the couples that do best after retirement are those where the partners retain the traditional roles. The husband may return to work, even if only part-time, while the wife remains at home keeping house. However, it may be that these studies are simply reflecting a particular generation, and that as the baby-boomer generation moves into retirement, they will break the mould for this as they have in so many other areas of life.

Those who seem to find it hardest to adjust to retirement are those men who retire completely from full-time work. They go from a full-on job to full-on retirement, often with little preparation. They are most at risk of becoming depressed, and even having a previously good marital relationship does not necessarily protect them against this. This may be because women who retire can easily expand their housekeeping role to give them a sense of purpose and being needed, even if they subsequently do other things as well. Men are less likely to slip comfortably into this role. Indeed, this can be a problem when the wife continues to work and expects her husband to do more now that he is at home, while he still considers that housework is her job. A number of studies in the past have shown that emancipation has still not progressed very far into the realm of responsibilities for housework.

Deciding How Much Time to Spend Together

There is a danger, too, that the newly retired person may expect too much from their existing partner, and these expectations can also put a strain on this relationship. This can be a particular problem where one partner retires after the other, and where one has been a full-time home-maker. The one who is used to being at home will probably have established a way of life that does not include having their partner around all the time, and he or she may resent having to make changes.

Most people need some time alone and space to themselves. Some people need more than others, and if you are someone who needs a lot of time alone then you need to be honest with your partner about this. It may be that your working life gave you opportunities to be alone which being at home full-time will not. Be aware that this could become a problem and plan accordingly.

It sometimes happens that a marriage or relationship will have survived reasonably well while both partners were working. Each might have their own life and circle of friends, and it is only after retirement that it becomes apparent that the marriage is not as sound as it may have seemed. It is relatively easy to avoid conflict if you do not see much of each other, and thus you may never really develop the skills for resolving difficulties between you. This is particularly sad if it leads to the breakdown of the relationship at a time when most couples are planning to spend more time together. Nevertheless, if a relationship is really failing, it may be better to accept this and move on. Before taking such a drastic step, however, do consider seeking professional help. A good therapist may be able to help you resolve what feels like a stalemate, and if you can manage to do this, your relationship will subsequently be healthier and stronger. Indeed, even if you do not feel that you are at risk of splitting up, seeking help from someone who can look at the situation objectively can be a real help in resolving any problems that do arise.

It is important to try and avoid getting stuck in the past, rehearsing old resentments. Try to think about retirement as a new phase of life and an opportunity to make changes. Think about how you would like your life to be in the future and see if you can negotiate some improvements. This applies both to your relationship with your partner, and to your relationships with other family members.

Finally, do try and avoid being dependent on each other. Many couples have developed ways of living together that mean that they lack skills in an area that the other one sees as their own. As you enter retirement and old age, you need to accept that it is very probable that one of you will die before the other. The one who is left will need to have the skills to cope alone. Both of you, therefore, should have an understanding of your financial affairs and be able to manage them alone. Both of you should know the basics of home management and be able to clean and maintain the house, or know how to get help to do so. Both of you should also be able to do enough basic cooking to survive and provide yourself with a healthy diet. If this is not the case, then one of the first tasks of your retired life should be to teach your partner any skills that you have in these areas that they may lack.

Working Together

It may be that one of the plans that you have always cherished is the idea that when you retired you would run a business together. A favourite choice used to be to run a bed and breakfast establishment in a seaside resort. Before you embark on making a plan like this happen, you need to give serious thought to how well you are going to be able to work together. There are many couples who spend a large part of their married lives working together, running businesses jointly, and this never causes any major problems.

However, if you have always had separate working lives, you may need to renegotiate your relationship in order to work happily together. For example, is one of you better at dealing with financial matters? Should that person always have the final say in the decisions that are made about the business? Are you going to employ others? If so, who is better at managing other people? If running a bed and breakfast means that the woman in the partnership has to do all the cooking, cleaning and washing, this is hardly a fair division of labour. If you would really like to take on a project like this, you need to do some careful planning and have some honest discussions with each other before you begin. If you each make a list of your strengths and weaknesses in a work setting you can then discuss how you can best use each other's strengths in a working partnership.

Negotiating With Each Other

I have mentioned previously the need to be honest about your feelings and to state clearly what you want. You need to learn to be assertive, if you are not already. Being assertive is often misunderstood and many people confuse it with aggression. Aggression means bullying people into doing what you want, while assertiveness is about honest expression of feelings, and negotiation. Sometimes it is as simple as being able to say no.

In order to say no, you do not have to shout, or even raise your voice. You don't have to be unpleasant in any way. You simply have to be firm, and say 'No thank you, I would rather not do that.' Many people find this surprisingly difficult. They worry that they will upset or offend people, or be thought unkind or difficult. While all of these are possible responses, quite often people will simply accept what you say.

If your retirement period is going to be a success, then you need to develop the skills to ask for what you want, and refuse what you do not want. It is no use going along with what your partner wants all the time, if the result is that you become resentful and frustrated. Neither is there any point in whining, complaining or acting the martyr. You need to state your position firmly and stick to it.

One psychological approach (Transactional Analysis) proposes that we function in one of three roles with other people; we operate as the parent, the adult or the child. Some people tend to get stuck in one of these roles, and rarely or never use the others. Most of us switch around, often depending on how others treat us, or indeed how we feel at the time. Ideally, as adults, we should be trying to operate in the adult mode as much as possible.

For example, a wife might say to her husband, 'I saw a lovely dress in the local shop today. Please can I have it? I have worked so hard lately, I deserve it.' This wife is operating in child mode. Her husband might reply, 'Of course, my darling, you have been an angel this week. Let's go down there now, and I'll buy it for you.' If he does, he is operating in parent mode. Equally, however, he might say, 'No, you can't! You know that we can't afford it. How can you be so selfish, when you know I need some new clothes much more than you do?' With this response, he has also slipped into child mode. If, however, he were to respond as an adult, he might say, 'Well, we have both been working hard, but you know we agreed not to spend any more money this month. Things are a bit tight, and we need to be careful for a bit longer.'

Couples tend to develop patterns of interaction which favour one or more of these modes, and they are not always healthy. Someone who operates a lot of the time as a child needs to grow up! They are avoiding responsibility, and putting the entire load on to their partner. Equally, someone who is always operating as a parent needs to accept that others may have opinions which need to be considered. An adult-to-adult communication is always a healthier one because both partners are then taking equal responsibility. In the above example, the wife's adult response might be, 'Yes, I know you are right. I did really like the dress, but I suppose I don't really need it.' If she stays in child mode, however, it might be, 'Oh, you are so mean. You never let me buy things for myself.'

Think about your interactions with your partner, or indeed with anyone close to you, and see which modes you operate in most often. Try and think about how you might change more of your communications into the adult form, rather than child or parent mode. You may need the help of a therapist to enable you to do this, but there are some good books around that may help too.

If you find that your partner is putting forward a particular view very forcibly, then clearly this is something that is important to them. If you are going to avoid conflict, you need to hear what they are saying and understand. Sometimes, it is tempting to jump in with an automatic response because you feel you already know what they are saying and know what the problem is. This can be self-defeating. If someone feels you are not really listening, they will tend to repeat themselves and get annoyed. Try to get into the habit of listening carefully to each other. Develop the skill of reflecting back to make sure you have really understood. This means repeating what you believe they have just said, in your own words: 'So you think that we should get rid of the car now?' Then wait for them to confirm that this is correct before you reply. They may surprise you by saying, for example, 'No, I am saying that we should think about it in the spring, if we find that we are not using it very often.'

If you have discussed an issue many times before, it may be that you feel you have already stated your views and your partner should know them. If this is the case, you need to ask yourself why he or she is returning to it. What is the issue behind this concern? Often, you will find that there is an unexpressed idea that is driving them, but which has never been clearly or openly acknowledged. By slowing down, and taking time to listen properly, you may find you are able to communicate at a new and more helpful level than before, and come to a real solution. Don't shout your partner down or bully. By taking time to listen you may be surprised at how differently you feel about the discussion, and you may finally come to a solution.

Most arguments between retired couples seem to centre on how money is spent, the need for time alone or space apart from each other, and sharing household duties. The question of whether or not to move house can also cause some difficulties, especially if one partner has always had a dream of moving to the country or seaside and the other wants to stay put. If such issues are not to spoil your retirement years you need to grasp the nettle now, and decide on a plan that works for both of you. Inevitably this may mean that you have to give way on some things that ideally you would like. Try and work out solutions where you both win, wherever possible. While compromise can sometimes be a solution, it can sometimes mean that neither party really gets what they want from the situation.

What is a win-win solution? Well, for example, if one partner wants to move to the seaside and the other does not, it may be possible to find a solution where the couple have a caravan or motor-home, and spend more time by the sea than they used to do. Or perhaps they could buy a holiday home, if finances allow, and spend a significant part of their time there. While there is a degree of compromise here, a solution like this means that both partners get a reasonable share of what they really want.

Re-evaluating Your Relationship

In the hurly-burly of working life, you and your partner may have slipped into roles or ways of being together which are not ideal, or which do not really fit with your retirement. Whether one or both of you is retiring, and whether one of you has been a full-time home-maker, will have a significant effect on how your relationship develops during the early retirement phase. Sadly, for a few couples, this can be the final blow to an already shaky relationship. Fortunately, most couples find this is a good time, when they can spend more time together and share interests.

Make sure that as retirement approaches, you both understand and accept the necessary changes to your relationship and your way of life. It is important that you are both happy with what you agree, and that it works for both of you. If not, then tensions will develop, and arguments and unhappiness will follow.

If your styles of communication have not been ideal in the past, maybe now is the time to try and improve them. Work on being honest and open with each other, and you will both benefit. Good relationships require good communication, and equality. No relationship will flourish if one party is always giving way to the other, or feels bullied or unheard.

Finding Someone New

If your long-term relationship has failed, or your partner has died, it may be that one of your dreams in retirement is to find someone new. More and more older people are finding new partners to share their final phase of life, and there are many more ways now to meet new people. If you do find a new partner you will need to think carefully about whether you will marry or not, as this can have significant financial implications, especially for those who stand to inherit from you. While it may seem unsavoury to discuss money while in the first flush of romantic attachment, it is something you will need to consider before you make any serious commitment. Pensions may be affected, and there will be issues around inheritance of property. You will need to make a will, or revisit an existing one, to ensure that you are dealing with everyone fairly. It is wise to get some professional advice.

Adult children can sometimes be disapproving and critical of new partnerships. Often these feelings have their roots in resentment that someone else seems to take the place of a beloved parent. If you think this is the case, try to discuss this with your children and reassure them that this is not so. Each relationship is different and each will have its own merits. They may also be worried that they are going to lose financially if you remarry. The extent to which you wish to reassure them on this matter is largely up to you. Children who genuinely care about your welfare are probably going to be pleased that you are happy above all else. You should not allow your children to bully you if you are sure that you have found the right person.

However, do beware of dismissing all their concerns. If you have more than one child, and they are all expressing concern about the new partner, then try and step back from your emotional attachment and see if they have a point. Is it possible that this person is after your money or property? This is an unpleasant question to have to ask yourself, but an important one. Do not be rushed into anything. Anyone who truly cares for you will wait.

Be very wary of rushing into a new relationship too soon after bereavement. Studies of loss, as described earlier, suggest that it may take up to two years to grieve fully for the loss of someone close, and in some cases it may be much longer. There is a temptation to fill the empty space as quickly as possible with someone new. Men seem to take this approach more often than women, and it can be disastrous for both parties. When you have lost someone you need to come to terms with life on your own again, and to accept that they have gone.

Anyone else that you find is not going to be the same person as your spouse. That may sound obvious, but often people fail to realize this until they are faced with the difficulty of adapting to a new person with different ways. Grieving is painful, and it is only natural to try and avoid pain. However, unfortunately, to grieve effectively you need to feel the pain of loss and work through it. If you don't do this, then you will not be able to settle happily into a new relationship. There is even evidence that a failure to grieve properly can have long-term effects on both your physical and your mental health. There are organizations that offer help to the bereaved and it may be very helpful to talk to someone sympathetic about your loss. Indeed, sometimes it is sharing their feelings about such losses that may bring an older couple together.

Try to make sure also that you and your new partner both have the same ideas about this new partnership. Many couples in their later years continue to enjoy active, if slightly more leisurely, sexual relationships, while others are happy to let that part of life go. A significant proportion of men become impotent as they get older, or at least have occasional problems in that department. This can be the result of medication for a physical condition, such as high blood pressure, or it may be emotional in origin. Physical causes of impotence, however, do increase with age and it is important that if you have a problem, you are honest about it. Men still find it difficult to talk about such things, even to a doctor, but it is not fair to a new partner to deceive them if you know that this part of your life is probably over.

Similarly some older women are very happy to let their sexual life come to an end, and may not wish to resurrect it with someone new even if they welcome kisses and cuddles. Honesty, as always, is the key, and the discussion needs to happen before you make any real commitments, not afterwards.

The Best Years of Your Life

If you can negotiate this apparent minefield of potential problems, you may find that the retirement years are among the happiest of your life. Most couples who have weathered the storms of mid-life crises and teenage children will find that their relationship is stronger than ever. While there may be a few sad partings during this period, most couples who have got this far without separating will stay together for the duration.

Retirement offers opportunities to spend more time together, to share new and old pleasures, to make new friends and enjoy old ones, and to spend more time with family members. It can be a time of new beginnings, of relaxation and removal of pressures. While problems may still remain, especially those of limited income and failing health, with care and planning you may have a significant chunk of life left to enjoy. Your partner is someone that you chose because you believed they were special, and you now have more time than ever to enjoy this person's company.

Don't forget, however, that almost everyone benefits from some time alone, and that keeping at least part of your lives separate can keep your interest in each other alive. Needing time apart does not mean that your partner does not care for you. If you hate being alone, then plan to spend time with others when your partner wants some space. There are always other people who will want and need your company and you may be able to do some good at the same time. Look on this retirement phase as the time when you can make the very best of all your relationships and you will find that your enjoyment of your retired life increases accordingly.

7

Health

The current generation approaching retirement is extremely fortunate. We are probably healthier than any generation before us and are likely to live longer, on average, than any previous generation. We have better medical care, and a better understanding of what is required to maintain good health.

Nevertheless, as we get older, many of us begin to suffer from a range of health problems, often chronic. In addition, there is often some decline in hearing and sight, and even in the sense of smell. This is not so surprising. Using once again our analogy of the older car or other machine, the system will show evidence of wear and tear, and if it is to keep on working in the way we want it to it needs regular maintenance and careful use. You would not expect to be able to treat an old car like a new sports model, and it may help to think of your body as an ageing car and treat it in the same considerate way. However, many chronic health problems can now be managed much more effectively than in the past. New medications can help to control conditions such as diabetes and high blood pressure, and difficulties with vision or hearing can often be cured or minimized.

As with cars, some of us have the good fortune to have

better models than others. Much of this is down to genetic inheritance. We now know that many conditions have a genetic basis which predisposes us to develop them in certain circumstances. We all have our strengths and weaknesses. Whether or not we actually develop a given disorder will also depend on a number of factors – some chance, but many related to lifestyle. There have been many studies looking at health and diet, as well as other aspects of lifestyle, such as exercise and smoking. Unfortunately, there are some contradictory findings, and in some cases the relationship between the disease process and the lifestyle choice is not well understood. Nevertheless, what is clear is that excess in any area is not helpful, and that some aspects of our modern lifestyle are definitely damaging to health. Smoking is one of these. To enjoy the best of health in your retirement you would be well advised to stop, if you are still smoking.

It may be that you are one of the unfortunate people who had to retire on grounds of ill health. If so you may be thinking that this is all too late for you. While it may be too late to change the fact that you have a condition such as cancer or heart disease, it is still the case that how you proceed from here onwards can affect the course of your disease, and may prolong your life. Stress-related conditions, such as high blood pressure or an ulcer, will usually improve once the source of stress is removed, and in some cases may disappear altogether. Problems that are related to pain and joint disorders may also improve with careful management, and the one thing that you now have is time to look into the best ways to manage your condition.

Physical Health and Activity

Good health thus depends on genetic inheritance, diet (both past and present), adequate rest and sleep, regular exercise and lack of stress. Stress is a topic that could fill a book on its own, and much has been written about stress and its management. Stress also has a bearing on psychological health.

We have already noted several times that physical activity should be part of your overall retirement plan. Why is this important? Well, the one sure way of losing your physical strength and fitness is to stop moving around. It has been estimated that for every day that you spend lying in bed, if you are ill, you lose 3 per cent of your muscular strength. If you take to your bed and stay there, it will not be long before you are unable to do very much at all, whether you are actually ill or not. Similarly, if you want to maintain your fitness, sitting in a chair all day is not the way to do it. Muscles need to be used. If they are not, they will waste away and become weak.

If you have back, knee or other joint problems that give you pain, you may be tempted to sit or lie down for long periods to try and reduce this. However, ultimately, lack of activity will make things worse, not better, because joints will stiffen even more and the muscles that support them will become weakened. The best strategy in this situation is to get up and do something active for a short period, and then rest. Alternate your periods of activity and rest, without pushing yourself to the point that the pain is excessive, but keep moving at regular intervals and resting in between.

If you have a disability that means you have to spend a lot of time in a wheelchair, then it may be even harder to try and keep fit. However, it is still important to try and keep your body as fit as you can. It may be helpful to talk to your doctor about what resources are available in your area. In some parts of the country there are regular physiotherapy classes for those with physical disabilities to help them maintain as much fitness as possible.

Even if you do not have such problems, it is easy to develop a sedentary way of life after retirement. To maintain physical fitness it is wise to ensure that you spend some part of each day doing something that is physically demanding. This might be a walk to the shops, or around a local park, or it might be an hour or two of gardening. If these are not possible then most communities now have a sports centre and gym available, and these will have a range of activities on offer. If you enjoy sport, then perhaps a session playing your favourite sport two or three times a week will help. Generally it is better to keep exercise to the gentler end of the spectrum as you get older. Walking, cycling, swimming, moderately energetic gardening and so on are probably better than jogging or squash, which tend to overtax the joints. Some people do, however, continue with demanding sports. There have even been marathon runners in their nineties. However, for most of us, it does seem that exercise that is gentler does less damage to joints and ligaments. It is also better to exercise regularly and moderately, either daily, or two or three times a week, than to do a large amount only once a week. It is important not to overdo things as you risk suffering an injury. Remember that as you get older you heal more slowly.

Research studies have shown that those who walk at least a mile a day tend to live longer than those who do no exercise. In some cases this was as much as ten years or more. Walking is probably the best exercise you can do as an older person. It is good for you, not too demanding on the body, cheap and enjoyable. It can also save you money if you walk instead of using buses or the car. Physical exercise is also good for your mental health, and research has shown that it can be as effective in treating depression as drug treatment.

If walking does not appeal to you, then consider something like yoga or Pilates. Yoga involves gentle stretching and flexing of the body and is marvellous for maintaining flexibility. Pilates focuses on posture and correct muscle usage to maintain the core body strength. Swimming is also one of the best forms of exercise for older people. If you can't swim, how about seeing if you can join a class and learn?

Setting up a good exercise routine is often hard to do alone. If you can find a friend or partner to exercise with you, in a pleasant place, you will be far more likely to do it. Afterwards you can reward yourself with something pleasant, so that in addition to feeling virtuous, you have a pay-off in other ways too. Sharing a coffee with a friend after your exercise class might be a good example. Maintaining your level of physical activity is about developing an exercise habit. Those who have always been active tend to stay active. If you have not been an active person previously, it may take a little while to cultivate the habit.

The Importance of Diet

In recent years it has become much more widely accepted that we are what we eat. Your food is the fuel that your body needs to run and to repair itself. Eating food that is polluted, heavy in fat and sugar, or otherwise unhealthy, means that your body has to work much harder to perform effectively. Too much food is probably worse than too little, because if you eat too much food you will get fat, and this means that all the systems of your body have to work harder, especially your heart and your joints. Consequently, they are more likely to fail.

Over the last twenty years or so, we have been constantly bombarded by the media about risks from food, varying from polluted food, to food infected with various disease-promoting agents, and we are constantly advised of the need to avoid different types of food. For the average person, this mass of information about food risks has almost reached overload. It sometimes seems that we have been given so much contradictory information that it is difficult to know what to believe and what to eat. However, there does seem to be a consistent message that excess in any area will cause problems. Too much of anything, even water, can be potentially harmful. Furthermore, what also seems to be clear from this mass of studies is that processed food is not healthy. It is much better to buy fresh ingredients (better still to grow your own) and cook them yourself. That way you know exactly what has gone into the food you are eating.

A Balanced Diet

What is a balanced diet? If you are not sure, get yourself a good book on diet and food. Briefly, you need some protein foods like meat, fish, cheese, eggs or beans. If you are vegetarian, you need to eat a wider range of foods to make sure you get all the right kinds of protein. No single vegetable food contains all the proteins that you need, so to obtain what you need you have to combine different types of vegetables and grains. You also need carbohydrates for energy (bread, potatoes, rice and pasta are common examples) and a little fat for additional energy and generally to help your body function. Vegetable fats like nut oils or olive oil appear to be better than animal fats. Vegetables and fruits have a variety of sugars, proteins, minerals and vitamins, which are all essential for good health. It has now been accepted for many years that you should aim to have something from each food group each day, and current research favours having a minimum of five portions of fruit or vegetables each day.

As we get older, it becomes more difficult for our bodies to maintain themselves and repair damaged tissues. We also have more difficulty in fighting off diseases and recovering from them. Good food forms the building blocks of these defence and repair systems. Older people often get into bad habits in terms of their diet, partly because they don't want to bother cooking a proper meal for one, and partly because they have limited money. Often, too, their appetite is less good than it was. Over a long period of time, bad food habits like this can lead to chronic malnutrition, which makes them vulnerable to developing other diseases.

If you live alone, it may be hard to motivate yourself to cook for one. There are two ways to tackle this. Raw food is good for you and is much quicker to prepare. Salad, cheese, fruit and bread is just as good as a cooked meal of meat and two veg; indeed it is probably better for you. Alternatively, if the weather is cold and you would rather have hot food, consider making a large pot of soup or stew to keep in the fridge or freezer, and eat it over a few days. If you are not a great lover of vegetables, this can be an excellent way to get your daily allowance in disguise. A small soup blender will turn them all into a pleasant thick soup which is filling but low in calories. The addition of good bread, and maybe a bit of cheese, will make this an excellent meal from a nutritional perspective.

Watch the Alcohol

Most of us enjoy a drink from time to time. Alcohol is pleasant, relaxing and enjoyable, especially when consumed in a social setting. However, alcohol is a dangerous drug. Because it is so commonly used in our society, we tend to disregard the risks. It is addictive, it causes serious health problems if taken to excess over a long period, and under its influence people act in ways that they would otherwise never do. Alcohol is linked to domestic violence, violent crime and road deaths. It arguably causes far more human misery than many illegal drugs, if you consider the sheer numbers of people who abuse it regularly.

Long-term users of excessive alcohol can suffer from liver disorders, and in some cases the brain will be affected. Excessive alcohol use can lead to a particular form of memory loss, which is associated with poor nutrition. People who drink excessively tend to eat poorly, and their brains suffer from vitamin deficiency. Too much alcohol can also lead to depression, and an increased likelihood of suicide. For some people it aggravates chronic anxiety, and these people are prone to becoming seriously addicted. They drink to reduce their anxiety, and when the effects wear off they are even more anxious than before, so they drink more. Alcohol can also disturb healthy sleep patterns. Although it may initially help a person sleep, its effects soon wear off, and regular or heavy drinkers often wake in the night. Also, if you drink regularly your body gets used to alcohol, so you need more and more to get the same effect. This is what makes alcohol an addictive drug.

However, the good news is that a small amount of alcohol, taken regularly, can actually improve your health by reducing the risk of heart- and blood-related problems. Red wine has been shown to be particularly good. Beer drinking, however, is less healthy, and excessive beer drinking has been linked to colon cancer.

Bear in mind also that alcohol is a diuretic, which means that it encourages the body to excrete more urine. This means that it dehydrates you. Make sure that when you have been drinking alcohol you drink plenty of water afterwards. This will stop you having a hangover. Dehydration is a common cause of confusion in older people, and can even lead to death. A good habit is to alternate drinks of water and alcohol.

How much alcohol is too much? Medical opinion about what is a safe amount keeps changing, and women are more susceptible to the effects of alcohol than men. Not only are they smaller, but their body contains more fat, so the concentration of alcohol in their blood, glass for glass, will be higher. Recently, the standard recommendation has been no more than two glasses of wine or one pint of beer per day. The problem here is that wine glasses have become much larger in the last few years in the UK. (A wine glass measure used to be 125 millilitres. In pubs now, it is often twice that.) It is probably safer to go for the smallest measure when you can.

If on one night you drink a lot more (because you have visitors, for example), then you should abstain on another night. If you find yourself drinking in the morning because you feel you need to, or finishing a bottle of wine a day on your own (or worse still, a bottle of spirits) then you have a problem. Even if you feel OK and you think that it does not affect your performance in any way, you are putting your health at risk and you have a problem which is getting out of control. You will probably need some help to bring it under control, and it is a good idea to discuss it with your doctor. Similarly, if someone close to you is expressing concern about your drinking, you should step back from it and be honest with yourself. Is it getting beyond your control? If you feel that you must have a drink every day, then you probably have a problem. If you are drinking because you are worried, depressed or lonely, then it would be better to try and get some help for the underlying problem rather than resorting to alcohol.

Keep a Check on Yourself

One of the ways that you might help to maintain your good health is by having regular checks from your doctor. Conditions such as diabetes or high blood pressure often present few symptoms, if any, in their early stages, and as you get older it is wise to have a check for these from time to time, especially if you have a family history of such problems. Your doctor may also want to check your cholesterol levels and your kidney or liver functions. Views differ about the best way to manage cholesterol levels and it may be wise to discuss this with your doctor. Don't be pressured into taking medication, though, unless you are convinced there is really a need to do so.

Many older people end up taking regular medication for a chronic condition, and you should be aware that this can pose its own risks. Doctors are busy people and may not always have the time to discuss fully with you the implications of the drugs they prescribe for you. Do your own research and make informed decisions about your health-care. Older bodies process medications more slowly and less effectively than younger ones, so it makes sense to minimize the medication that you take. Avoid taking regular painkillers, and it is probably also unwise to use sleeping tablets on a regular basis. If medicines are out of date, *do not take them* – return them to the doctor's surgery for disposal, and never take a drug that has been prescribed for someone else, especially if you are already on medication. The effect could be lethal.

Older people can sometimes become confused about medication and take the wrong amount, or forget to take some tablets. If you need to have regular medication, it is important that you understand why you need to take each drug, and what it is supposed to do. Although it can be alarming, it is wise to read the enclosed leaflets so that you know about possible side-effects and can look out for them. If you are uncertain about what your tablets are for, don't be afraid to ask your doctor or chemist to explain. After all, it is your body, and you have a right to know why you are being asked to take a particular drug.

You also have a right to refuse it if you are worried about possible side-effects, or find them unpleasant. Beware, however, of just stopping a drug without telling your doctor. In some cases this can be dangerous. Stopping medication for high blood pressure, for example, can cause a stroke. Some drugs need to be reduced or stopped very slowly and carefully if you are not to suffer any ill effects.

Notice any changes in your body, its appearance or the way it works. Often these are harmless and just part of normal ageing, but sometimes they can signal that things are going wrong. If you have any recurrent symptom that worries you, see your doctor and discuss it with him or her. If you are not happy with the response you get, then see another doctor, or insist on a referral to a specialist.

Mental Health

The division between mental and physical health is a totally artificial one. Poor mental health can affect you physically and vice versa. Stress can lead to high blood pressure, ulcers, heart disease and even cancer. Depression can affect your sleep, digestion and physical appearance, as well as increasing the risk of death from suicide. Often, when people refer to mental health, what they are actually thinking about is mental illness. Good mental health tends to be taken for granted. The mentally healthy person is happy, relaxed, content with their life, and confident that they can cope with what life throws at them. While they may experience anger, frustration, sadness or even despair at times, they are resilient enough to deal with these emotions and regain their equilibrium fairly quickly. The person with poor mental health, in contrast, will often be anxious, depressed to the point of being unable to function effectively, worried about every change that happens, stressed, bad-tempered with those around them, or even suicidal. Where there are serious mental health problems, there may even be a loss of contact with reality. Problems may be exaggerated out of all proportion to the actual situation, and in extreme cases the person may be controlled by things they see and hear which are self-generated, that is, hallucinations.

Depression is common in the elderly and has its roots in a number of problems; loss of a partner, loss of friends through death, feeling socially isolated, loss of independence and physical health, and lack of money may all contribute. Many people experience a period of depression after retirement while they adjust to the changes, but this usually passes. Dementia in its early stages can look like depression, and people who do have dementia may also be depressed, so the picture can be confused.

People who have a previous history of mental health problems are more prone to develop problems in retirement. Their treatment, especially ongoing drug treatment, should be regularly reviewed as they get older. If you, or your partner, have such problems, it is probably sensible to see your doctor and ask him or her to review your medication now that you have reached retirement age. You may need less medication, or there may be new drugs that will suit you better.

If you suffer from mental health problems of any kind, don't suffer in silence. Talking through your problems with someone you trust can be enormously helpful. If you have nobody that you can easily talk to, then think about asking your doctor to refer you to a counsellor. Counsellors are trained to help people understand their current problem and work towards a solution. There is no shame in asking for this kind of help, and it may make a real difference to your process of adjusting to retirement. Taking on new roles and new activities can often help alleviate the less serious mental health problems. Sometimes all you need to do is make changes and you will find your mood improves. If you have had problems in the past, try to remember what worked for you then, and see if you can repeat it. Try to regard feeling down or depressed as a signal that something in your life needs attention, rather than as being a medical condition that needs drugs. While there are those who benefit from the additional support that drugs can give while they deal with their difficulties, drugs alone are rarely the long-term answer.

Maintaining or promoting good mental health requires attention in the same way that maintaining and promoting good physical health does. Dealing with stress, bereavement and other negative life events can be a real challenge, and it is worth exploring all possible avenues to help you through such events. Promoting a positive and active approach to problem-solving can make you feel more in control, and is likely to improve your mood and reduce your anxiety. Dealing with unhelpful thoughts in the ways already outlined can also be very helpful, and is essentially a strategy for developing good habits in your thinking. Regular exercise will not only keep your body fit, but will also help to improve depression. Finally, a good diet can even reduce the risk of dementia.

Dementia

Dementia is perhaps one of the most feared conditions of old age. Alzheimer's disease is probably the most common form, but its age of onset is usually quite late, often not until people are in their eighties. However, it can strike earlier in life and its effects at any age can be devastating, both for the sufferer and their families. There will be a gradual loss of memory and abilities, often including word-finding problems, and eventually the person will need full nursing care before they finally die. The progression of the illness varies enormously, however, and some people can live many years with the condition, while others may die within a couple of years. Although poor memory can be a symptom of dementia, the majority of elderly people suffer some deterioration of memory and problems in word-finding, so these are not diagnostic symptoms in themselves. If you are worried about the possibility that you may be developing dementia, then you should consider asking your doctor to refer you to a specialist as diagnosis is a complex process.

There are several different types of dementia, some which may appear earlier in life. Many of them have a genetic component, that is, they are partially inherited from our parents or grandparents; but it is also possible to develop a type of dementia as a result of a series of 'mini-strokes' if you have high blood pressure which is poorly controlled. Apart from the genetic component, the causes and/or triggers for the various kinds of dementias are far from clear.

Sleep

Sleep is important in maintaining good mental and physical health. It has been known for many years that lack of sleep can affect a person's mood, concentration and ability to resist disease. Some studies have suggested that chronic sleep deprivation can lead to psychosis or even death. The functions of sleep and dreaming are not well understood, but there is evidence that sleep is necessary for tissue repair, and dreaming appears to be necessary for healthy mental functioning.

Many people find that they need less sleep as they get older. Typically, a person in their twenties may need at least eight hours a night, while someone in their sixties may feel fine on only six or seven hours. However, there is a huge amount of individual variation, and some young people may be happy with three or four hours' sleep, while some older people still need eight hours. Although older people generally need less sleep, they need it more. In other words, they cannot do with less than their ideal amount of sleep as easily as a younger person can. The young can party all night and sleep all day, whereas older folks need to get to bed even if they are up at six the next morning.

Early waking is a common symptom of old age, and can be trying. Many older people find that in addition to waking early, their sleep pattern is unsettled, so that they wake more frequently in the night than they used to. This is often caused by a need to go to the toilet, but once awake they find it hard to get back to sleep again. Those with chronic pain problems may also find their sleep is restless. There is often a temptation to resort to sleeping tablets, although doctors are less willing to prescribe these than they used to be. This is just as well, because most of the commonly used sleeping drugs are addictive in some way, and some of them have rather unpleasant after-effects when you try and stop them, such as anxiety or nightmares.

If getting to sleep is a problem, avoid eating large meals or drinking coffee late at night, and you may find that limiting your intake of fluids after nine o'clock can help the bladder problem. As already mentioned, a small amount of alcohol may help you go off to sleep, but a large quantity will probably ensure you wake up during the night. Also, if you do this regularly, it may lose its effect. If you are a man and find you are having trouble passing urine, or you feel you cannot empty your bladder properly, see your doctor as soon as possible because you may have prostate problems. See your doctor too if you need to pass urine a lot and are very thirsty all the time – you may be diabetic.

Pre-sleep Routines

What is the best way to promote good sleep? First, establish a good sleep routine. Try to go to bed around the same time, and get up around the same time. While the occasional late night or lie-in will do no harm once a pattern is established, if you have no pattern at all, then your body will never develop a healthy sleep habit.

You will also never be able to sleep well if you are excited, tense or anxious. In order to develop a healthy sleep pattern, you need to work out a routine before bedtime which enables you to wind down. People often find that working or playing on the computer until just before bedtime means that you go to bed with your mind whirring and it is difficult to switch off. Similarly, sitting up watching exciting or scary films just before bedtime may make it hard to relax afterwards. Having a warm bath before bedtime and spending a bit of time just pottering around, reading a pleasant book, or listening to music can be enormously helpful in calming the mind and relaxing the body. You may also find it helpful to buy one of the many commercially produced relaxation audio tapes or

CDs, which you can listen to in bed just before you go to sleep. (Health food shops often have these, or your local library may be able to help.) These will teach you a routine of relaxation which will help you to drift off. If you have some earphones, you can also repeat this process in the middle of the night when you wake up, without disturbing your partner.

This approach can be particularly helpful if you suffer from chronic pain that makes it hard for you to get off to sleep, or if you suffer from tinnitus. As a tinnitus sufferer you are probably used to the idea of masking your ear noises, but learning to relax using a recording like this will have a double function. Other useful techniques to help you relax fully are meditation or self-hypnosis. These can also be used to help you control chronic pain, or the noises of tinnitus. Such techniques take a little longer to master but can be learned from books or CDs and can be very effective. Other ways to learn are by joining a group which meditates regularly. Often yoga classes will include some meditation exercises.

If all else fails and you simply cannot get to sleep, then the best thing to do is to get up for a while, or put the light on and read. Of course, if you sleep with a partner, this can be more difficult, because you risk waking them too. However, if they are sound asleep, it may be possible to creep out without waking them and go into a different room. It is also now possible to buy small LED book-lights which give out a tiny focused light on to your page, so you can read without disturbing others. Another possibility is to use audio-books on your tape, CD or MP3 player and listen rather than read. This is also helpful if you have either visual problems or tinnitus.

If you do get up in the night, avoid coffee and anything too stimulating that will wake you up even more. Read a gentle, perhaps amusing book, or watch a bit of TV (not exciting or scary films though). Try a hot milky drink – some people swear by a mug of hot milk as a sleeping aid. If the weather is cold, then make sure you don't get chilled – wrap up well and put a heater on. Make yourself comfortable, and after a while you will probably find that you will start to feel drowsy again. At this point you can return to bed and try your relaxation exercises again, or you may even find that you fall asleep where you are. If you decide not to return to bed, make sure that you are wrapped up warmly, in case you do drift off.

One of the worst aspects of sleeplessness is that people tend to worry about it. It is not helpful, or likely to promote sleep, if you lie there getting more and more frustrated about not sleeping. This is why getting up for a while is recommended. If you catch yourself thinking things such as, 'I shall feel dreadful tomorrow if I don't get my six hours in', or 'This is awful, every night I lie awake like this', then use the same approach as we discussed in chapter two. Try to challenge those thoughts with more positive ones, such as: 'I have had four hours good sleep, and if I relax I shall probably drift off again soon', 'If I can't sleep tonight I shall have an afternoon nap tomorrow', or 'If I don't get much sleep tonight, I can go to bed a bit earlier tomorrow and catch up then'.

If you are regularly having trouble sleeping, then it may be worth considering what you eat and drink during the day. Coffee is a well-known stimulant, and some people are very sensitive to caffeine. For some people even one cup is too much. Try cutting it out for a few days, and see if your sleep improves.

Similarly, as already acknowledged, alcohol can cause sleep problems in some people. While it may send you off to sleep at first, once the effect wears off, you may find that you wake up in the night feeling anxious and wide awake.

Even sensitivities to food can cause sleep problems in some people. However, this is a complex area and you might need to seek the services of a specialist in this area to identify what is causing your problem.

The worst thing that you can do is to convince yourself that you have a serious sleep problem, and label it 'insomnia'. Sleep is a habit to be cultivated, and although there may be times when yours is disturbed take comfort from knowing that this is not abnormal in later life. Plan some strategies for coping so that you feel more in control. Lying in the dark staring at the ceiling and feeling like a victim will not improve your sleeping, and you will feel even worse in the morning. If you go to bed convinced that you will not sleep, then you probably won't. If you have already got into this negative loop, then start tackling it now. By setting up good, healthy sleep routines, you will minimize the amount of time that you lie awake fretting. However, you also need to accept that as someone who is getting older you probably don't need as much sleep as you used to do and you are more likely to wake in the night. Once you can accept this and plan accordingly, you may find that you can feel more relaxed about your sleep, and will probably sleep better too.

Mental Fitness

We have considered how best to maintain good physical and mental health. However, it is also useful to include in your retirement plan some ways to maintain mental fitness. This means trying to keep your mental faculties at their best. Most people accept that there will be some decline in their mental faculties as they get older, but this is not necessarily universal. Unless you are unfortunate enough to develop dementia, it is possible to continue to have a lively, agile mind until the day you die.

Those who seem most able to maintain their mental agility into old age are usually those who have always had an active mind. Brighter people tend to maintain their ability level for longer. However, whatever your starting point, it helps to maintain your interests and to seek out new ones. Lack of activity and giving up all mental challenges seems to have a negative effect on the brain. Like the rest of the body, if it is not used, it will deteriorate. Recent studies have suggested that those who continue with brain-stimulating activities on a regular basis are less likely to develop dementia than those who do not. At its simplest, reading or doing a crossword or Sudoku puzzle every day can be a good way to keep your brain fit. Alternatively, take up a new hobby such as bridge or chess, learn a language or enrol for a course of study. Anything that provides your brain with a challenge will help to keep it working well. Continuing to work or taking part in education also appears to help keep the brain active and fitter.

Memory tends to decline with age in almost everyone, but regular use and exercise can help to minimize this loss, and the development of simple strategies such as a calendar or diary where you can write down important appointments can really help to avoid some of the frustrations of forgetfulness. If you are someone who tends to put things down and lose them, then it can help to try and return important items such as keys or glasses to the same place every time you put them down. This means you will always know where they are.

If you need to remember some new information, then repeating this over and over again is the best way to get it into your long-term memory. This strategy tends to work best if you do it little and often, so, for example, if you want to learn your French verbs for your new French class, then read them regularly every day for a week or two. You are more likely to remember them this way than if you try and sit down for a couple of hours to learn them in one go. This technique works well for younger people too.

Sometimes it is easier to learn new information if you can link it to something you already know. Older people may have an advantage here because they have had more experiences and probably learned more throughout their lives, so they are more likely to be able to find an earlier piece of information to make the link.

Coping With Long-term Health Problems

If you are already unwell, and your illness limits what you can do, it may seem hopeless to plan or hope for anything better in the future. Adapting to retirement alone can be a challenge, but if you are also faced with a life that is limited by a physical disability or illness, then this can be doubly daunting. Studies have shown that approximately one-fifth of retired people have had to retire on health grounds, and about half of one retired group who were asked said that they no longer had the energy or health to continue working. Loss of health and energy seems therefore to be a common problem for older people.

Chronic health problems are not unusual in the later years. Many people find that they develop high blood pressure, diabetes, sight problems or deafness as they get older. Some have arthritis or other joint problems, which make movement painful or difficult. Others are even more unfortunate, and will have been diagnosed with heart disease, cancer or dementia. While it can be very alarming and upsetting to find that you have developed such a condition, all the above suggestions about physical and mental health are still valid. It may be that you will need to be more careful about what you choose to do, and it would be wise to discuss your plans with your doctor. Nevertheless, the principles still apply; a degree of exercise will help muscles to remain fit and healthy, and the maintenance of positive patterns of thinking and mentally challenging activities will help to keep your brain working at its best. Even if you have been told that your life expectancy is now limited, you will still be likely to get the best out of your remaining time if you look after your mind and body as best you can. You may even extend the period remaining to you.

Fortunately most of the chronic health problems associated with old age can be managed reasonably well with the help of modern medical techniques. If you find you are faced with a new diagnosis for a condition that you know little about, then you would be wise to carry out some research. We have already noted the importance of knowing as much as you can about your condition. Many family doctors will supply you with written information about common conditions, and there are some excellent publications available which can help you to understand your problem better. It pays also to familiarize yourself with possible drug treatments, so that you can make informed decisions about what you want to take, and what you don't. All drugs have some side-effects, although fortunately not everyone is affected. If the drug you are given does not agree with you, then if you know what the alternatives are you are better placed to discuss with your doctor what might suit you better.

Beware of doing a lot of research on the internet. While there are some excellent sites that may give you valuable and up-to-date information, the quality of information on the internet is very variable and in some cases downright misleading. Be suspicious of anyone who is peddling a cure. They clearly have a vested interest in convincing you that you need their product. The best information is likely to come from independent medical sources, such as university medical schools and hospitals, or from charities which have been set up to inform and help those with a particular condition.

Pace Yourself

If your condition makes you tired, or movement is painful, then the most helpful strategy that you can use is that of 'pacing'. This has been used for many years in the treatment of those with chronic pain, or chronic fatigue. The idea is a simple one – any activity should only be done for relatively short periods, and in between there should be periods of rest. If pain is a problem, then your activity should stop *before* your pain becomes unbearable. Stop and rest, say for half an hour, and then do some more. As your muscles become stronger, you will usually find that you can gradually increase the period of activity, until you may be able to carry on for an hour or more without severe discomfort. If your pain level does not change, then simply alternating periods of rest and activity will ensure that you maintain a degree of physical fitness without causing excessive pain. Painkillers can help, especially in the early stages of establishing this pattern, but it is wise to limit your use of these as far as possible. Some can become addictive, and many of them cause stomach and bowel problems, so long-term use is not advisable.

Typical problems with this approach are that the person tries initially to do too much. At first, your periods of activity may need to be very short, perhaps only a few minutes long. Once your pain level has increased to the point where you simply have to stop, you have overdone it, and it will take longer for your body to recover. You need to be disciplined and stop before you get to that point. This is one of the hardest things to do. As a species, we seem to find it very difficult to leave a task unfinished, and people feel driven to carry on, desperate to finish what they have started. If you do a job in small parts and stop before you are in agony, the job will still get done and you will not suffer nearly as much pain. Over time, you should find you can slowly increase the length of the time that you are active, without getting to the point of excessive pain.

Another common difficulty is that the person's thoughts get in the way. Thoughts such as 'This is pathetic, I can't even mow the lawn in one go', or 'Surely I should be able to walk round the shops without having to sit down every few minutes', are not helpful. Sometimes people worry that others are staring at them or thinking they are odd. It really does not matter what other people think. They have not got your problem and they cannot feel your pain. You need to develop the habit of looking after yourself. Once you do this, you will find you can do a lot more, even if it is at a slower pace.

If your problem is fatigue, then you can operate exactly the same approach, but for you the measure should be that you stop before you are so exhausted that you simply cannot do any more. Otherwise the process is exactly the same as above, and you should be able gradually to increase what you can do without suffering a setback. If you do overdo it, you may find that you suffer a significant setback and for a while can do even less than before. This can be very alarming and discouraging, although it will pass. However, try to avoid this happening by taking things gently, especially at first.

If you work on focusing on what you can do, rather than

what you can't do, you may surprise yourself. People who have been physically disabled for some time can often be very inventive in finding new ways to do things that they used to do, and often they will decide to try something completely new. You may need to adopt an unconventional way of doing things, but that is the challenge. If you have lost the use of your right hand, experiment with what you can do with your left. If your eyesight is too poor to read, then experiment with talking books. Very often the major obstacle in taking this positive approach is not in developing the skills, but in overcoming the mindset that leads you to focus on the negative. Once again, we are back to the idea of challenging negative thoughts and trying to replace them with more positive ones. However, unless you also change your behaviour, you will not believe that doing things differently can work for you. It may be inevitable that age and illness bring some losses, but this need not mean that you have to give up completely. Even if you are in a wheelchair there are always ways that you can contribute, and in the process you can enjoy life, whether by working for money or by volunteering.

Experiment and test your limits – you may be pleasantly surprised. It is important to realize that whatever your physical limitations there are still things that you can do which will be rewarding and challenging. You may not be able to contribute in the same way as those who do not have these health problems, but there will always be some things that you can do. Try to develop the habit of being inventive and creative, and see how you can work around the problems that you have. Above all, learn to look after yourself in every way.

8
Overview

This chapter tries to bring everything together and show how this can lead on to your next phase of life in a positive way. It also discusses how you are now going to plan and organize for your retirement years, and the need to stop and evaluate your progress every so often. It also looks at how other issues, such as housing, money and family responsibilities, can help or hinder the development of this new life.

As we have examined the various aspects of retirement and what it can mean for you, we have constantly returned to two main themes. One is that you need to know yourself, and the other is that the quality of your thoughts determines the quality of your life. Recently we have heard a lot about 'you are what you eat'. This is both important and true, but what is also true is that you are what you think. Negative patterns of thought breed misery, depression and frustration. If you consider your life is now over and you, as a retired person, are worth nothing, then that is what you will experience and you will not enjoy your retirement. If you work on taking a positive approach to the problem of adjusting to retirement and experiment with new activities, new friends and new ideas, then you will begin on a phase of life which is both exciting and rewarding, despite the limitations that age brings to all of us.

Many people currently retiring have not really appreciated exactly how long they could live, and what a large part of their overall lifespan this retirement phase could be. It is a terrible waste of such an opportunity to spend it focusing on what you can't do. Try not to be tempted into thinking things such as 'Is it worth trying to do this at my time of life?' Remember, you may still have ten, twenty or even thirty years of life left. Even if you haven't, if you fancy trying something new, then why not try it? Of course, poor health or fitness may limit what you can do, but if you work on looking at what you can do, rather than what you can't, you will find that your state of mind becomes much more positive and you may be surprised at what you can achieve.

Think about others you know who are already retired. Is there anyone who you would want to use as a role model? If there is, look at what they are doing to make their retirement work well and see to what extent you can model your own retirement on theirs. If you have no obvious role model, then instead you can begin with a plan that could, for example, include making some new friends, having a range of activities, and doing something that makes you feel useful and worthwhile.

There is a real danger of being overtaken by depression and despair in the later years, as your body begins to show signs of age and there is an increasing frequency of friends and acquaintances dying. The loss of a life partner can be particularly difficult to handle. In addition, there is a possibility that as an older person you may regret things you have never done, or indeed some that you have done, and may even wonder if you should have taken a different course through life. It is important to fight this tendency, because it can rob your final years of a great deal of enjoyment. Of course you need to grieve for what you lose, and this is a process that cannot be avoided. However, it is also important to maintain a sense of future and not give up.

Many older people feel ready to disengage from the world of work, and some will happily retire to what seems like a very limited, even barren lifestyle to someone younger. However, the key to whether you are succeeding in your retirement should be your own state of mind. If you are content and enjoying life, then that is what counts.

It is also quite common that as people get older they want to review their past life. They may decide to visit old haunts, perhaps old homes or places that they went to school. This is quite usual, and seems to be part of the process of adjustment to getting older and making sense of a past life. If you feel you want to do this, then do not feel that this is odd or unnatural. It is part of your personal adjustment and may be really helpful.

Readiness to Retire

Are you now ready to retire? Have you given careful thought to the issues discussed so far? If you haven't started yet, how about setting some time apart when you can be undisturbed, and tackling this as a project just as you might have done at work?

Begin by carrying out a financial review. Find out what you are worth, what your pension will be worth, and what you need to live on. If moving house or area is part of your plan, then do some very detailed research into the likely costs and benefits of your plan. Once you have done this, you will know whether you need to include some kind of employment in your overall plan or not. Until you have done this, you cannot really think about the other aspects of retirement.

Get to Know Yourself

By answering the various questions that I have posed throughout this book, find out who you are and what you want. Make a list of your strengths and weaknesses (honestly), and another list of your interests and dreams. Using the ideas outlined, you should be able develop a reasonably clear picture of yourself and the kinds of things that are likely to make you happy and contented. Until you have done this, it will be difficult to make informed choices. You will be much more likely to develop a plan that works for you once you know yourself well.

Some people seem to want to slow down, and to develop a more leisurely way of life, while others want to keep up an active and demanding lifestyle. Both are valid choices but which one you choose relates to the kind of person you are, and what you consider as most important to you. By following the suggestions made in earlier chapters, you should be able to decide what is right for you, and plan accordingly.

Relationships

Take a long, hard look at all your close relationships, and decide how well they work. If they are not working very well, then try and decide how you might improve the situation. The first step in this process is to communicate with the other people concerned and listen to what they want and need too. Your retirement plan will not work well for you if it makes those close to you unhappy or dissatisfied. Look at ways in which you might improve communication between you, and acknowledge that each of you will need space and time apart as well as together. Learn to be assertive, but also to listen.

Above all, spend some time cultivating those friends whom you want to keep and try to find new opportunities to make new friends. You have more time than ever to give to those you care about, so make the most of it. You will probably find that many of your relationships improve and grow as a result of this extra time given to them. If you live alone and have no close family, then it is even more important to get out and meet others.

If you find that you have family responsibilities, such as caring for elderly parents or your partner, or looking after grandchildren, do try to set realistic limits on these. It is tempting to avoid seeking help and to feel that it is your duty to do everything, but this is not wise. You have to remember that you may not have the stamina and resilience that you once had, and if you push yourself too hard, then it is likely that you will become ill.

It is also worth remembering that caring for someone who is becoming increasingly dependent is very hard work. It may result in broken sleep and additional stresses, as well as the sheer physical effort involved. If you have help, or the person spends some time being cared for elsewhere, you will share the load and have time to recharge your batteries. When you do have to return to your duties, you will be more relaxed and will probably do a better job than if you had tried to struggle on alone.

Moving on Emotionally

You need to accept that things will change and work on being able to cope with any changes and adapt to them. However you decide to plan your retirement, there will be some changes, and it is no use burying your head in the sand and just hoping it will all go away. You also need to accept that some of this process of adaptation may be uncomfortable, even painful. This is part of life, and you need to be able to tolerate this discomfort for a while in order to make your adaptation successfully. The more you can plan and organize your future life, the less threatened you are likely to feel when the process actually begins.

Try to get a clear idea of what kinds of things make you feel fulfilled, happy and successful. Decide which of these were fulfilled by your job, and then try and work out ways of finding alternatives. If company is important, then look at how you can get out and meet others, both old friends and new acquaintances. If structure or status were important to you at work, look at how you might find alternative ways of achieving these while retired. If you need to feel useful, then caring for others or volunteering may be right for you.

Moving House or Not?

This is perhaps one of the biggest retirement questions. It can also be a real source of tension between couples, if one wants to move and the other does not. For many people retirement comes with a dream of moving to a little seaside town, out into the country or abroad. Once you no longer need to worry about living near your work, moving somewhere more attractive and peaceful can be very appealing.

Unfortunately, living the dream is not always as enjoyable as you might imagine. However mundane your usual surroundings, the chances are that you have friends and neighbours nearby, and you have built up a network of people, facilities and activities which are important to you. Moving some distance away will disrupt all of this, at a time when you are faced with many other changes as well. In addition, when you are older, you are less likely to find a new network of friends quite so easily. It will take a lot of time and effort to build up a network such as you already have in a new place. If you have friends or family already in the new area, then this may make it easier. Beware of moving to a seaside town where you have only had holidays in the past. Living in such a place full time may be a very different experience. Holiday destinations, for example, can be very quiet and dull out of season.

Be careful also, of taking on a property that is hugely appealing when you are a fit sixty-year-old, but ten years later might become a burden. If you love gardening, it may seem wonderful to take on a huge garden when you first retire, but ten years later when you are feeling less fit it may become a real struggle to manage it. Then you will be faced with another move, which may be even more of a challenge at that stage.

Another reason to move house when you retire may be that you are worried about being able to cope with your present house in the future. It may be old and need ongoing repairs and maintenance, or it may simply be rather large now that the children have grown up and left home. Perhaps it has lots of stairs or a large garden, and you are already concerned you may not be able to manage them as you get older.

However, think carefully before giving up the family home. When you are at home all the time, extra rooms may come in very useful for hobbies, or for family visits, which may now be more frequent. Also, many people feel that it is rather negative to dwell on the problems of old age while you are a hale and hearty sixty- or sixty-five-year-old. Ultimately, it is a matter of personal choice. Some people are reassured by taking all these precautionary steps as soon as they retire. Others would view them with horror, and feel that they would be giving up to even think about such things before they really need to. Once again, this comes down to who you are. If you are inclined to be a worrier, and are cautious by nature, such preparations may help you to feel more comfortable. If you are a risk-taker and don't want to accept that you will change as you get older, then you are more likely to want to keep going as you are for as long as you can. There is no right or wrong here. The choice is yours.

The last reason for moving is financial. You may be able to resolve any financial difficulties by selling a large house and realizing some of the capital. This may make the difference between needing to keep working or not. Bear in mind, though, that selling and buying houses is an expensive business these days, and you are likely to lose several thousand pounds of your profit in paying the costs of the move. You may also consider moving from an expensive area to a cheaper one for the same reasons. As with moving to the seaside or countryside, think carefully about such a move before you commit yourself. If money is the sole reason for moving, you may do better to look into one of the equity release schemes that are now on offer. However, these are a very mixed bag, so do get good, independent financial advice before taking a step like this. As before, the right choice for you will depend on what kind of person you are. Those who are happy to take risks, and who are naturally more outgoing, will probably find such a change exhilarating, while more cautious or introverted individuals may find it all too stressful.

Increasingly older people are making their retirement moves into retirement villages or other sheltered housing developments. This can be a very good move for anyone who enjoys company, and who fears that they may need more help as they get older. However, these communities can present their own problems. It may be much harder to move out again if you find that the place does not suit you. The other residents may not be to your liking, or you may find that you prefer to have less company and more privacy. For some people these are an excellent choice, but do carry out some careful research before you commit your life and your cash to such a venture. Moving when you retire is a big step, and the decision should not be taken lightly or impulsively. Assuming that you and those close to you are in agreement, do some detailed fact-finding before you go too far.

Constructing Your Plan

By now you have probably answered all the questions, thought about your likes and dislikes, and begun to feel, perhaps, that you are ready to retire. Once you have done this, you can begin to put together your plan of action. In the first stage, begin by returning once more to those five requirements of a good retirement:

- Social contacts
- Physical activity
- Intellectual challenges
- Creative activities
- A passion – something to get up for

Once you have worked out the various parts of your retirement, and tried to match them with the five requirements as listed above, you should be able to write out your plan for your retirement. This can, of course, change in the future, and it is a good idea to review it regularly. However, your first draft could look a bit like this:

- Things that I already do
  - Play tennis once a week (physical)
  - Go to a French class once a week (intellectual and social)
  - Gardening (physical and creative)

- Changes I need to make
  - Get better at saying no, rather than being pushed into things
  - Plan to take up a new activity with my partner e.g. join a dance class
  - Draw up a spending budget and stick to it

- Things I would like to do
  - Travel to exotic places (intellectual, social and physical)
  - Spend more time with the grandchildren (social)
  - Take up pottery (creative)
  - Study history (intellectual and social – if I join a class)

- Things I might like to do, but am not sure
  - Become a school governor (intellectual and social)
  - Learn to dance (physical, social and intellectual)
  - Take up flying (physical, intellectual)

Some of these activities will bring you into contact with new people, and some will provide you with some social responsibilities, which can be good for your self-esteem and sense of worth. If you are uncertain about a course of action, then look for as much information as you can before committing yourself. If possible talk to people who have done it before, and see how they found it. If all else fails, then have a trial run. Make it clear to the people concerned that you are not sure, but would like to try things out first. This will be easier in some activities than in others. However, if you have to commit yourself to a given course of action, then tell yourself that it will be for six months or a year, and then review it. If you decide it is not for you, then there is no reason to continue.

At the end of all this, you should have a fairly clear idea of what you are going to do with your retirement, and be able to summarize it in a sentence or two. It is not, of course, set in stone and indeed you should aim to review your plan regularly, perhaps once a year. A good plan will consider all the aspects of your life, and ideally will aim to be a long-term rather than short-term plan. Remember that retirement is not just a longer-than-usual holiday; it is a whole new phase of your life.

If you see gaps in your plan after considering all the above areas, then aim to fill them. However, beware of committing yourself too deeply or too soon to something completely new. Try to allow yourself a period of experimentation first. If you are very unsure about your plan, then you may need to begin with several short-term plans with a view to developing more long-term ones, once you have tested the waters in a few new areas.

It is also wise to think about your stress levels, and manage the demands on your time accordingly. In the first flush of enthusiasm about your retired status, you may be in danger of taking on too much and ending up as stressed and exhausted as you were at work. Sometimes, those who have had a busy life feel that they must hurry to fill all their time once they have retired. Remember, excessive stress tends to lead to health problems, and one of your main aims as a retired person is to preserve the best level of health you can. The better your overall health, the more you will be able to enjoy your retirement phase. So, take new things on slowly, bit by bit, and ensure that you can manage each addition comfortably. Practise saying no if you have not been good at doing so in the past. Avoid being pushed into things that you would rather not take on, and if you really feel you have no choice (for example, in caring for an ailing family member), do try to set some limits on what you do, and ask for help if you need it.

Taking Things Step By Step

It is tempting to feel that you need to solve the problem of retirement in one go. If you are a goal-directed person, who has been used to getting lots of things done, you may want to sit down and sort out a retirement plan today. There is no harm in doing this, but you may well find that in a few months' time you need to make changes. A more successful approach is likely to be a staged one. You will begin with a tentative plan and try things out. Some of your ideas will work really well, and some will not. This does not matter. What is important is that it works for you and makes you feel that life is enjoyable, worthwhile and stimulating. If you are in a long-term partnership, it needs to work for your partner too.

Over time your health may change, your financial situation may get worse or better, or you may discover a new passion. Any of these kinds of changes will lead you to want to change your plan. The arrival of grandchildren where there were none can make a huge difference to your life. In addition, many people find as they get older that they want to disengage a little from life. Their world seems to shrink, not necessarily in a negative way, but simply because they do not have the physical and emotional energy they used to have. If you begin to find that your retirement interests are becoming as much of a burden as perhaps your work once was, then you may need to take stock and reduce what you do.

Be guided by your own feelings, not those of others. You know how you feel better than anyone else. If you are still full of energy at eighty and want to learn to fly, then why not? If all you want to do is be at home and enjoy your home and garden, then do that instead. We are all different and there are no rights or wrongs here. The advice given in this book aims to maximize your enjoyment of your retirement, not bully you into a way of life that you do not want.

Do I Need a Therapist?

If, despite your best efforts, you still feel confused or unhappy about your retirement, maybe you should consider getting the help of a professional therapist. Just because you are older and retired, this does not mean that therapy is not for you. This kind of help can make an enormous difference to how you feel, whatever your age.

It is not always easy to decide whether you need help from a professional therapist. Often, if you are honest with yourself, you know deep down what needs attention in your life, but you are reluctant to face the challenge. Sometimes, you may feel trapped by circumstance. Lack of money, or the needs of those who are dependent on you, may stop you from taking a decision that would benefit you. You may be well aware of this but avoid taking that decision because the consequences feel impossible to contemplate. In this kind of situation, a therapist may be helpful in clarifying the issues for you, and perhaps suggesting options that you had not considered. However, if you have the right kind of close friends, who will listen and help you to make the right decision for you without imposing their own views upon you, then they may be able to give you all the help you need and you probably do not require a therapist.

If, however, you are beset with vague feelings of anxiety and depression that you feel unable to analyse, or you seem to be locked into a cycle of conflict with someone close to you, it may be very helpful to talk to someone who is completely outside your circle of family and friends.

Similarly, if you find that you are trapped into unhelpful patterns of behaviour that you keep repeating, such as overeating, drinking too much, gambling or drug-taking, a therapist may be able to help. If you are so miserable and depressed that you cannot get out of bed in the morning, then you definitely need help, probably both medical and psychological.

What Will a Therapist Do?

We have already discussed how you might begin to become aware of negative and unhelpful thoughts that may be trapping you into patterns of distress. The basics of cognitive behavioural therapy (CBT) were also described. Often people can understand these ideas quite quickly and make use of them for themselves. Many therapists now use the principles of cognitive behavioural therapy to help people to change the way they think, and thereby change the ways they feel and behave. For many, this approach is both helpful and effective. It also has the benefit of promoting relatively rapid change. Unlike some of the other techniques used, it does not require months or years of treatment and can often help significantly in a few weeks.

In the case of feelings of depression resulting from retirement, you may be asked to plan to go out and join a new group of people or take up a new activity, in order to challenge any thoughts you may have about being useless or unwanted. Again, it is very important that you do try out these new things, because unless you make changes in your everyday life, your mood is unlikely to change.

Cognitive behavioural therapy (CBT) can be very helpful for those who like structure, because it is a very structured and goal-directed form of therapy. It has a clear rationale, which can be explained fairly easily, and it seems to benefit many people fairly quickly. If you are struggling to cope with your newly retired state, and are beset by unhelpful and negative thoughts, this may be a very helpful form of therapy for you.

Other Types of Therapy

Other therapies include counselling, rational-emotive therapy, Gestalt and Transactional Analysis (TA) and psychoanalytic psychotherapy. Most of these will only be available privately. An internet search should help you to identify practitioners in these areas, but do make sure that they are properly registered and qualified.

In the UK, it is now relatively easy to see a counsellor who may be attached to your GP surgery and in many areas CBT is now increasingly available. However, you should be aware that the quality of the training of those who call themselves 'counsellors' can vary enormously. Training in counselling can vary from a few days or weeks to years of supervised practice. If in doubt, approach a professional organization such as the British Psychological Society, who should be able to recommend reputably qualified counsellors in your area. A good counsellor will work in a variety of ways, and may employ a range of theoretical approaches, but essentially the counsellor should be there to help you solve your own problems.

If you are struggling with adapting to retirement, and are feeling anxious, depressed or otherwise unhappy, then it may help you to talk to someone independent about this. If your relationship is suffering, it may be helpful for you to see a counsellor together, preferably one who specializes in relationship counselling.

Final Thoughts

The current generation of people entering the retirement phase of their lives are in a unique position. We have seen that they are probably healthier, fitter and better educated than any generation before them. While many of them may have one or more chronic health problems associated with ageing, thanks to the development of medical care these people can still expect to live longer than their parents, and as a result their retirement has become a significant phase of their lives.

You are fortunate enough to be one of these people. You are blazing a trail which has not been followed before. This book aims to help you do this in such a way that you get the most out of the remaining years of your life. Whether or not you need to continue to earn money, you can still make a real and useful contribution to society, and enjoy yourself in the process. Retirement is not a short space of time between finishing work and dying. It is, for many of us, a substantial part of our lives, and we should plan to make it useful, satisfying, productive and, above all, fun.

Further Reading

Consumer Publications, *Approaching Retirement* (Which Books, 1989).

Ellen Freudenheim, *Looking Forward; An Optimist's Guide to Retirement* (Stewart, Tabori and Chang, New York, 2004).

Jim Green, *Your Retirement Masterplan* (How to Books, Oxford, 2004).

Michael Longhurst, *The Beginner's Guide to Retirement; Taking Control of Your Future* (Newleaf, Ireland, 2000).

Rosie Staal, *Earning Money after You've Retired* (White Ladder Press, Devon, 2007).

Eric Sundstrom, Randy Burnham and Michael Burnham, *My Next Phase; The Personality-Based Guide to Your Best Retirement* (Springboard Press, New York, 2007).

Useful Websites

Great Britain

Inland Revenue, for tax information – www.inlandrevenue.gov.uk

The Pension Service offers advice on pensions – http://www.thepensionservice.gov.uk/state-pension/home.asp

Experience Corps, for volunteering – www.experiencecorps.co.uk

Age Concern (charity with a range of services) – www.ace.org.uk

Age-Net (site for a range of interests for the over-fifties) – www.age-net.co.uk

The Oldie (specialist magazine) – www.theoldie.co.uk

North America

Celebrating life over fifty in the USA – http://www.eons.com

Training, employment and community service for older people in the USA – http://www.experiencecorps.org

A general resources site for over-fifties in the US and Canada – http://www.genplususa.com

A resources site for those retiring in Canada – http://www.canadaretirement.info

Australia and New Zealand

A general resources site for those who have retired in Australia – http://www.aussie-retirement.com.au

The Australian Government's information site for Australians over fifty – http://www.seniors.gov.au

A government information site for visitors to Australia considering retirement – http://www.immi.gov.au/visitors/retirement

New Zealand's Best 50+ Community Site has a section on retirement – http://www.grownups.co.nz/list/lifestyle/retirement

The Retirement Commission assists with financial planning – http://www.retirement.org.nz

There are many, many more, but this selection will get you started.

Index

Index